CONSTITUTION, CULTURE & NATION

CONSTITUTION, CULTURE & NATION

KALRAJ MISHRA

PRABHAT PAPERBACKS

Published by
PRABHAT PAPERBACKS
An imprint of Prabhat Prakashan Pvt. Ltd.
4/19 Asaf Ali Road,
New Delhi-110002 (INDIA)
e-mail: prabhatbooks@gmail.com

ISBN 978-93-94534-25-4
CONSTITUTION, CULTURE AND NATION
by Shri Kalraj Mishra

Edition
First, 2022

Translation
Kunwar Kanak Singh Rao

Price
₹ 350.00 (Rupees Three Hundred Fifty Only)

Printed at
R-Tech Offset Printers, Delhi

These articles have been published from time to time in various dailies and magazines like Dainik Hindustan, Rajasthan Patrika, Dainik Bhaskar, Amar Ujala, Lokmat Samachar, Rashtradoot, Mahanagar Times, Punjab Kesari, Dainik Jagran, Indian Express, Times of India, Hindustan Times, First India, Pioneer, Outlook, Panchjanya, etc.

Thank you!

Author's Note

A nation is a living philosophy in itself. Whenever I contemplate the nation from the Indian perspective, I find it as a terrain associated with a sublime life-view. A land where there is no narrow view of caste, creed, opinion, and discrimination against human beings. Such is the Indian vision of the nation.

The constitution of the country that was written after the independence of the country has the echo of this very culture of the nation. The Indian Constitution is based on the values of equality and liberty to all irrespective of caste, religion, class, etc. This is our culture. The Constitution, culture, and nation are actually intertwined.

I believe that the nation becomes stronger only when its people are committed to following the values associated with the constitution and culture. Even though we got freedom from the British in 1947, the real freedom of the country means writing our own destiny. It is also important to uphold freedom. Upholding freedom means committing to fulfilling one's duties towards its nation and enjoying the rights written in our constitution. I like to call the 'Indian Constitution' a 'global document of human rights'. The reason being the perfect blend of rights and duties consisting the lofty values allied with life on which the development of humanity is founded, that is why awareness of the constitution is necessary. Awareness and understanding of the Constitution is the key to working for the culture and the national interest. That's why I took the initiative to establish a Constitution Park in the universities of Rajasthan. Its purpose is to bring together youth who will be shouldered with the responsibility of upholding the Constitution meaningful and true to its values. The young generation should make our democracy—which stands on the strong foundations of freedom, equality, justice, and fraternity enshrined in the Indian Constitution—meaningful.

This is a proud moment for the nation. The nation got an opportunity to chair a meeting in the United Nations for the first time under the leadership of Prime Minister Shri Narendra Modi. Every citizen should look out for chances where he/she can prove his/her patriotism and do something for the country.

Manushya is derived from the word ***'mann'***. If we have the mind ***(mann/determination)***, we can touch the sky. The nation is paramount, nothing else is more important – this should be our priority. Maharishi Arvind had said something important once, "Mind is a semicolon, not a full stop." Along his lines, I would like us to connect the mind with the constitution, culture and, spirit of the nation. We should strive to make the best of what is around us. The great men in our country and the lessons they have given us serve as are the guiding light of the path of life… We should advance by following the light shown to us by our country's great men.

The gist of culture is the creation of a refined and cultured man. Human culture builds a connection between men. There is a vastness in it. There is no baseness in it. Indian culture is based on the concept of *'Vasudhaiva Kutumbakam'* (the world is one family) and embraces the entire world like one big family. However, boundaries like religion, caste, color, and the urge to prove oneself superior are shading our vision of being one. Therefore, it is neccessary to keep returning to the constitution time and again to embrace our embedded culture and keep the values associated with our nation higher than any other feeling.

Through this book, I am handing over the articleswhich I had written from time to time on the issues related to the Constitution, Indian culture, and the nation to the readers out there. There is a very popular poem by Rabindranath Tagore –

Where the mind is without fear and the head is held high;

Where knowledge is free;

Where the world has not been broken up into fragments

By narrow domestic walls;

Where words come out from the depth of truth;

Where tireless striving, stretches its arms towards perfection;

Where the clear stream of reason has not lost its way

Into the dreary desert sand of dead habit...

Let us all move forward while contemplating the concerns related to the Constitution, culture, and the lofty values associated with the nation. I humbly, welcome your opinion on the articles compiled in this book.

— Kalraj Mishra

Contents

CULTURE IN THE LIGHT OF PEOPLE

MODERN VIEW OF CULTURE

CONSTITUTIONAL CULTURE

1.

Indian Constitution: Light of Rights and Duties

India is a union of states. After the country became independent, a big challenge faced by the constitution-makers was how to write the constitution for such a vast country in a short period of time. This challenge was finally met after consuming 2 years 11 months and 18 days of continuous hard work and sheer efforts. The drafted constitution was refined and presented before the people of the country.The constitution was implemented in the country keeping in view the Indian social structure. Our constitution took inspiration from constitutions the world over. Fundamental Rights from USA, Parliamentary System from Great Britain, Directive Principles of State Policy from the Constitution of Ireland, and Emergency Provision from the Constitution of Germany and the provisions of the Government of India Act-1935. All of these were included in the Constitution of India.

India, as a union of states, has one unified constitution for both the states and the country itself. The states also follow the unified constitution. The constitution provides answers to all arrangements of both the state and the nation. The constitution provides for a parliamentary form of government, the structure of which is federal with certain unitary features.

President is the constitutional head of the central executive. According to Article 79 of the Constitution of India, the Council of the Central Parliament consists of the President and two houses, known as the Council of States (Rajya Sabha) and the House of the People (Lok Sabha). There is a provision in Article 74(1) of the Constitution that there shall be a Council of Ministers headed by the Prime Minister to assist and advise the President and the President shall exercise his functions in accordance with the advice. Thus, the real executive power is vested in the Council of Ministers, which is headed by the Prime Minister.

The constitution is actually the supreme law of the country. Personally, I believe that this is the sacred document with the balance of rights and duties, due to which democracy can endure effectually. 26 November is celebrated as The Constitution Day in the country. The Constitution of the country was adopted on this day in 1949 and it came into force on 26 January 1950. It is significant that on August 29, 1947, the drafting committee of the country's constitution was established. Dr. Bhimrao Ambedkar was appointed as its chairperson. As it has been pointed out earlier, the constitution was written after closely examining all the constitutions in the world. On November 26, 1949, Dr. Ambedkar, the chairperson of the draft committee, completed the constitution and dedicated it to the nation.

The Constitution of India is considered to be the largest constitution in the world. It consists of 12 schedules. The draft of the Constitution was handwritten both in Hindi and English. It was not typewritten or printed. It was a handwritten constitution with 395 articles in it. It took 2 years, 11 months and 18 days to prepare it. The document was signed by 284 members of the Constituent Assembly on January 24, 1950, and was implemented two days later.

The Constitution of India is the basic legislation of the country. It includes the ideals and values of our civilization as well as the beliefs and aspirations that arose from our struggle for freedom. The Constitution is the embodiment of the collective conscience of the founders of our republic. It is basically an expression of the desire for the sovereignty of the people of India.

Even after the Government of India Act-1935, the position of the central government in India remained the same as it was according to the Act of 1919 because the federal provision of the 1935 Act was never implemented. Since autonomy was introduced only in the provinces, necessary changes were made in the methods and procedures.

The freedom struggle got a new direction from the

'Quit India Movement' of 1942 in the country. Thereafter, several attempts were made to transfer power and provide a constitutional framework for an independent India. As part of these efforts, the British Cabinet Mission arrived in India on 24 March 1946. The purpose of this mission was to help the Viceroy in establishing such a system in India by which Indians could prepare their own constitution. Emphasis was placed on the core issues of independence and the formation of a representative Constituent Assembly for the preparation of a future constitution without outside interference.

The Cabinet Mission presented its plan on 16 May 1946, laying down the principles and procedure for the preparation of the future Constitution of India. Many suggestions were made in this plan regarding the constitution of the Constituent Assembly and how it can be formed without any delay.

The Constitution was prepared based on certain suggestions: The allocation of total seats for each province in proportion to its population, shall be determined by adult suffrage in terms of one representative for ten lakh numbers or so. To divide the provincial allocation of seats among the main communities in accordance with the proportion of the population of each province. To provide that the representatives allotted to each community in the province shall be elected to the Legislative Assembly by the members of that community., These were some of the suggestions on which our democracy is running till date.

The basic of the constitution is mentioned in the preamble

of the constitution. This preamble fully explains the purpose of our constitution allied to Indian culture. The preamble says –

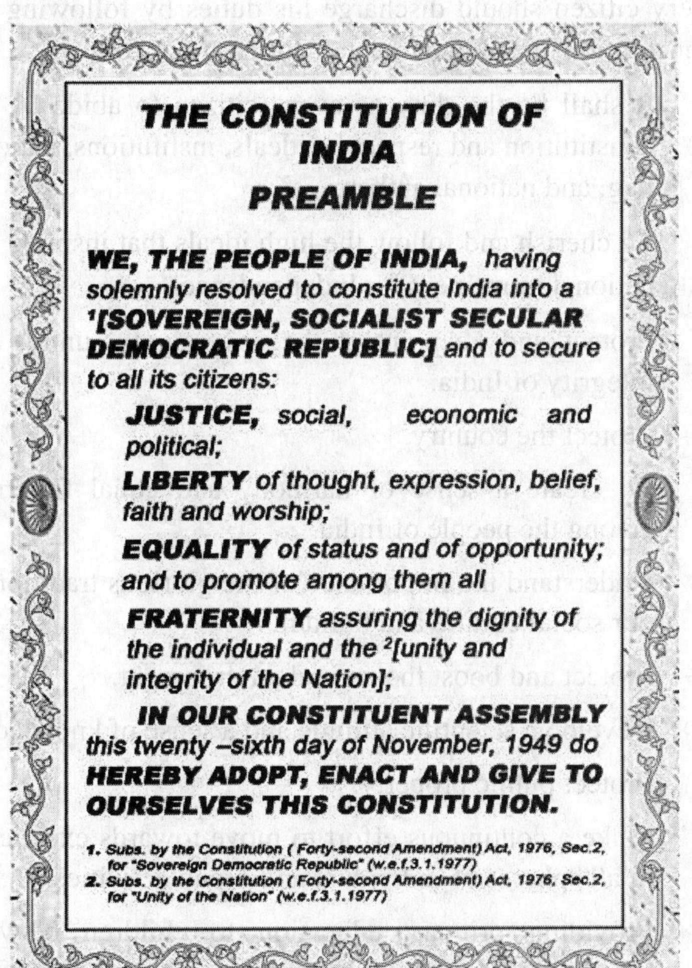

THE CONSTITUTION OF INDIA

PREAMBLE

WE, THE PEOPLE OF INDIA, *having solemnly resolved to constitute India into a* [1]**[SOVEREIGN, SOCIALIST SECULAR DEMOCRATIC REPUBLIC]** *and to secure to all its citizens:*

JUSTICE, *social, economic and political;*

LIBERTY *of thought, expression, belief, faith and worship;*

EQUALITY *of status and of opportunity; and to promote among them all*

FRATERNITY *assuring the dignity of the individual and the* [2]*[unity and integrity of the Nation];*

IN OUR CONSTITUENT ASSEMBLY *this twenty –sixth day of November, 1949 do* **HEREBY ADOPT, ENACT AND GIVE TO OURSELVES THIS CONSTITUTION.**

1. Subs. by the Constitution (Forty-second Amendment) Act, 1976, Sec.2, for "Sovereign Democratic Republic" (w.e.f.3.1.1977)
2. Subs. by the Constitution (Forty-second Amendment) Act, 1976, Sec.2, for "Unity of the Nation" (w.e.f.3.1.1977)

There are 11 Fundamental Duties mentioned in the Constitution. These fundamental duties indicate to the citizens, the culture of maintaining harmony along with maintaining the unity and integrity of the country. Under the Fundamental Duties of the Constitution, it is expected that every citizen should discharge his duties by following the Constitution. The Fundamental Duties are as follows-

- It shall be the duty of every citizen to abide by the constitution and respect its ideals, institutions, national flag, and national anthem.
- To cherish and follow the high ideals that inspired our national movement for independence.
- Protect and keep intact the sovereignty, unity, and integrity of India.
- Protect the country.
- To create a sense of harmony and equal fraternity among the people of India.
- Understand the importance of the glorious tradition of our social culture and build it.
- Protect and boost the natural environment.
- Develop a scientific attitude and a sense of knowledge.
- Protect public property.
- Make a continuous effort to move towards excellence in all spheres of individual and group activities.
- Providing primary education to children between the ages of 6 and 14 by a parent or guardian (86th Amendment).

Constitution makes us aware of our duties as well as

rights. As the constitution of the world's largest democracy, the Constitution of India is also a kind of global document of human rights. Respecting it means working for the dignity of our sovereign nation. There is a purpose why I have listed the fundamental duties and rights in this article. They aren't to be just seen, rather they need to be brought in practice. In a way, it provides light to live life. Think of it in such a way that these rights and duties allow you to play an integral role in the democratic system.

I also believe that when democracy fails in some places, the citizens of that country are equally responsible for it as the elected representatives are. This is because every citizen who believes in democracy cannot expect rights unless he performs his duties. The points that have been stated in the Preamble of the Constitution are in a way the essence of democracy. The light of democracy can be protected only by putting them into practice. Mahatma Gandhi had once said, "To me, democracy means a system wherein even the weakest section of the society gets the same opportunities as the most powerful section. In real democracy, power flows from the bottom up." In accordance with these lines, the Constitution transmits equality in democracy through rights and duties.

Indian Constitution is the vehicle of the healthy tradition of democracy. If we go into the values enshrined in the Constitution, it will also seem that it is inspired by the idea of building a society in which every person has the right to equality without any discrimination. It provides every individual with excellent opportunities for development according to his/her ability and talent. It infuses a sense of responsibility to protect the interests of the deprived sections and suggests an unceasing way of living life based on moral values. The discussion in the Constitution about living by moral values also has deep implications - if we explore its meaning, it will seem that the Constitution regulates such a system in which there is a resolve to protect the society and to serve its interests. What Babasaheb Ambedkar had said while presenting the Constitution is relevant even today. He had said that no matter how good a constitution is, it would eventually prove to be bad if the people who used it were bad. No matter how bad the constitution is, it will ultimately prove to be good if the people who use it are good.

Since the formation of the Indian Constitution, 127 amendments have been made to it so far. This flexible system has been kept in the constitution keeping in mind the situations, and needs that might change with time. The basic way of implementing the constitution is that those who use it should understand its limitations and remember the resolve to strengthen democracy. The rights and duties of the constitution are a reminder of this.

❑

2.

Universal Document of Human Rights

The constitution is the pride of our nation. What I experienced after becoming the governor and chancellor of universities in Rajasthan was that there was a lack of awareness among the youth about the constitution. The constitution is not only the ideal code of conduct for the country, but it is also an important manuscript that makes us aware of our duties and rights. That's why I took the initiative in Rajasthan that Constitution Parks should be established in all the government universities of the state. Under this, it was decided after discussions with the Vice-Chancellors of the universities that this Constitution Park should be made in such a way that every student taking admission to the University would become aware of the Constitution. The intention behind this is that our young generation should be aware of the process of running the democratic system of our country, the world's largest democracy.

I believe that the constitution is an important document that was written for the governance of the country and for running the state. It is the guiding beacon using which our democratic system operates. The Indian Constitution is the best interpretation of the democracies of the world. Along with the rights, it also makes one aware of civil duties one needs to fulfill.Therefore, constitution parks were created in all the universities of the state so thatour youth would be more connected with the basic spirit of the Indian constitution.

The work of writing the Indian Constitution started on 9 December 1946. Sachchidanand Sinha was the chairman of this assembly. Later Dr. Rajendra Prasad was elected as the Chairman and Dr. Bhimrao Ambedkar was elected president jurist. The framing of the Indian Constitution was completed in 2 years, 11 months and 18 days, and the Constitution of India was handed over to Dr. Rajendra Prasad on November 26, 1949.

The Indian Constitution is the accumulated reflection of the ideals, objectives, and values of our country and culture. The constitution is not a dead document, rather it keeps on evolving over time. Changes are made in it as per the requirement through a constitutional amendment; that is also the reason why the Indian Constitution is considered a prime example all over the world today.

Our constitution promotes the ideals of unity and nationalism. Initiatives should be taken in this direction to keep these ideals alive. the Constitution Park in the university was built on the lines of the same belief of inspiring the students to grow their democratic beliefs from an early phase.

The constitution is not just a document containing rules and regulations, rather it is a holy book. The Preamble of our country's constitution is considered to be the best in the whole world. It is clear in the Preamble of the Indian Constitution that the power of the Constitution is directly vested with the people. That is why our constitution begins with the words 'We the people of India'. The ideals and aspirations that the Constitution reveals can be understood clearly from the words 'We the people of India' in the Preamble of the Constitution. 'We the people of India' is not just a sentence. In a way, it is the philosophy of life of our great Indian culture where people and humanity are always first.

The Indian Constitution gives the right to social, economic, and political justice to all the citizens of the country. Our constitution also maintains its distinct identity around the world for freedom of expression, freedom of religion and worship, establishment of equality and fraternity ensuring the dignity of the individual and the unity of the nation in all.

I also believe that the Constitution of India is a universal document of human rights. If ever, there is a reliable system for the protection of human rights, then it is in the Indian Constitution.

Whenever I think of the Indian Constitution, I especially remember these lines from the poem of the World Poet Gurudev Rabindranath Tagore –

Where the mind is without fear and the head is held high;

Where knowledge is free;

Where the clear stream of reason has not lost its way

Into the dreary desert sand of dead habit...

These poetic lines of Gurudev are inspiring. Human rights and duties given in the Indian Constitution can be deeply understood in this poem. The Constitution of our country with its 'Unity in Diversity' is such an equality-based humanitarian system, in which everyone lives fearlessly and inspires the citizens to lead a life of high ideals.

There are civil rights as well as duties in the Indian Constitution. In Indian culture, there has always been an emphasis on establishing human dignity by balancing rights and duties. Mahatma Gandhi, the Father of the Nation had once said – 'From the Himalayas of duties flows the Ganges of Rights'.

The Indian Constitution also needs to be seen and understood from this point of view. Many times, I find that, though we are aware of the rights given in the constitution, we are indifferent to the duties. It is alright to fight and agitate for our rights and interests, but we should not turn rights into anarchy. We also need to know that fighting for one's rights can be constitutional, but under its guise, causing damage to the property of the nation, loss of life and property, breaking the law, damaging government buildings and properties is anarchy. This needs to be thought over deeply.

In a democracy, there should be an active intervention of the people for their own interests. The Preamble of the Constitution ensures this. However, this intervention should not be in the form of loss of public money or loss of national property.

The constitution is the boundary of freedom. Therefore, it is necessary that with constitutional values, morality, poise, and dignity, we respect the sentiments of the framers of the constitution while remaining free from hostility, hatred, and discrimination.

According to the constitution, it is the duty of every citizen to respect the constitutional institutions and follow the rules and regulations implemented by them. We must enrich the glorious traditions of our culture by upholding respect for all religions, maintain harmony, and the safety and dignity of everyone aound. It is the duty of every citizen to establish an egalitarian society in the country. The Constitution always inspires us for this.

The Indian Constitution is not only a human document of the balance of rights and duties, but it also has a very artistic form. I have perused the original copy of the Indian Constitution. I am proud to state that the Indian Constitution has been created in the form of beautiful artwork in the light of its constitutional provisions, human rights, and duties.

There are paintings related to Indian culture on every page of the original copy of the Constitution. The form of Nataraja is also inscribed on the original copy of the constitution, which is also the form of Maryada Purushottam Lord Rama and Lord Krishna giving the message of Karma. An image of Lord Buddha preaching peace has also been inscribed on the original copy of the constitution, while beautiful illustrations of sages performing Vedic *yagyas* have also been engraved on it.

It was decided that the constitution which was prepared under the guidance of Babasaheb Bhimrao Ambedkar should be a reflection of Indian civilization and culture.

The country's eminent artist Nandlal Bose and his students from Shantiniketan, therefore, made original pictures depicting the developmental journey of Indian history and not a particular religion. The national emblem Ashoka Pillar was placed on the front page of the Constitution, while the horses, lions, elephants found in the Harappan excavations were decorated with gold. The Preamble of the Constitution was decorated with these elements.

The famous artist Kripal Singh Shekhawat from Rajasthan was a disciple of Nandlal Bose. His art also adorns the constitution. I believe that it is a matter of great pride for Rajasthan that the art of Rajasthan has also contributed to the copy of the original constitution through Kripal Singh ji.

The original copy of the Constitution is handwritten in both Hindi and English languages. It was written by Prem Bihari Narayan Raizada. Raizada has written every page of the Constitution in beautiful italic letters with a pen holder nib. I believe the Indian Constitution not only serves as a written law for the operation of democracy but also as a book of pride reflecting Indian culture. That's why today on 'Constitution Day' I have recollected many references related to the Constitution.

The Indian concept of *'Vasudhaiva Kutumbakam'* believes in considering the whole world as one family. The Indian Constitution is a symbol of the Indian culture of unity in diversity and harmony of all religions and equality.

❑

3.

Cultural Bases of National Policy

The concept of nationality in our country India is based not on the state but the culture. In ancient times, there were separate independent states in different regions of India. But despite being divided into different states politically, culturally the whole of India has been considered a nation, which is the first example of its kind in the world. The basis of India's unity and integrity is its cultural unity. Therefore, the cultural concept of Indian nationalism and national policy are complementary to each other.

Indian tradition is not individual-based, rather it is society and nation-based. Here, the populace is considered above the individual. At present, the dominance of individual-based thought systems are presenting many dilemmas before society, country, and nature.

In national policy, from the point of view of cultural

basis, joint families also have their own importance. Though the national policy has a plan for the upliftment of nuclear families, it is the system of a joint family that strengthens this nation, which is absolutely necessary for the unity of this nation.

The only concern of a nationalist is the freedom and development of his nation. A nationalist person hates subjugation. His love for his nation is profound. He is ready to sacrifice his everything for the survival of the nation.

If we consider the inspirational points of Indian culture, then we will find that our culture has been liberal, appreciative, and syncretic. We are inextricably linked with the conductive principles of Indian culture, such as sympathy, imagery, behaviour, spirit, restraint, morality, generosity, and congeniality.

The conscience of Indian culture is intertwined with such a divine tradition that it is not possible for anyone to falsify it. Anyone can try to prove his innocence by citing many compulsions for his misconduct, but no one can dare call immorality moral. This is the reason why Indian culture has been called the timeless culture of the world. The abundance of commemorations, festivals, and birthdays and how they are celebrated with equal gusto is such a feature of Indian culture, with the help of which the entire society gets constant encouragement to keep adopting the traditions and get inspired by them. While fasting forms the background for effective treatment of abdominal diseases, there is also a sense of purification of the mind associated with it. Behind the association of *Agnihotra (havan)* with every auspicious occasion, there is also an inspiration for people to lead a sacrificial life.

Indian cultural philosophy has always worshipped nature. It says that while one should make proper use of natural resources, there is a clear prohibition on their exploitation. Perhaps, for this reason, we have a provision to worship trees and plants, rivers and ponds, fields and barns, animals and birds, wells and, in general, nature. from time to time.

There are also similarities in the rites conducted during birth, marriage, and death, customs, conduct, and festivals all over India. Despite the diversity of 1400 dialects and 22 officially recognized languages, the fundamental forms of music, art, literature, dance, and theatrical form have striking similarities. The seven *swars* of music and the *tritals* of dance are equal all over India. India is an ocean with rivers of many religions, sects, views, and different faiths and beliefs.

❑

4.

Indian Culture is the World Teacher

India has been occupying the position of World Teacher. We are all aware of this truth. Since thousands of years, our saints and sages have been busy in search of knowledge in various fields. There are many important contributions made by saints and sages to the world in the fields of knowledge and science, for which the whole world and society are forever indebted to them. The streams of knowledge in different fields have originated in India and are flowing throughout the world. Rigveda is considered to be the world's first book; Yajurveda, Samveda, and Atharvaveda were propounded after that. Vedas are considered equivalent to the voice of God. Lord Brahma is considered to be their creator. They have a vast store of knowledge related to every field.

India's literature is very rich and diverse. Apart from religion, philosophy, grammar, it has also contributed to subjects like mathematics, astrology, ayurveda, chemistry, metallurgy, military, science and so on.

Among the ancient masters of astrology, Aryabhatta holds a special place not only in India but also among the world's astrologers. In the fifth century itself, he had made the scientific discovery of constellations. He was the first to impart knowledge of the method of predicting the eclipse to the world. Acharya Brahmagupta, Varahamihira, Bhaskaracharya were also among the eminent astrologers of the world. Even today, in the *Panchangs*, the time of lunar eclipse, solar eclipse, moonrise, sunrise, setting and rising of Venus, Mercury and Jupiter constellations, which is written on the basis of Indian mathematical astrology, is completely true. Aryabhatta's *'Surya Siddhanta'* and *'Siddhant Shiromani'* are the finest books on astrology.

It is well known that zero and decimal were invented in India. It is an invaluable gift given by India to the world. There are mainly three parts of mathematics - Arithmetic, Algebra, and Geometry. Arithmetic was established in its developed form during the Vedic period. Yajurveda mentions numbers ranging from one to 10 trillion. The credit for the development of algebra goes to Aryabhatta. Geometry was also invented in the Vedic era. It has been learned from the study of *yagyashalas*, *vedikas*, *kunds,* etc. that their construction was based on the principles of geometry.

By the Vedic period, many minerals had been discovered and their practical usage had also started. Most of the work in this field was done by a Buddhist scholar named Nagarjuna.

The famous book called '*Rasratnakar*' on chemistry was authored by Nagarjuna. Texts like 'R*asahrudaytantra*', '*Rasarnav*', '*Ras-sar*'. are also famous Indian texts of chemistry.

In ancient times, the administrative system was religion-based. Major religious scholars like Vaishvanas, Atri, Ushana, Kanva, Kashyapa, Gargya, Chyawan, Brihaspati, Bharadwaja among others discussed the various principles and forms of religion. In Manusmriti, Yajnavalkya Smriti, Parashara Smriti, Narada Smriti, Brihaspati Smriti, all aspects of public life have been explained from the religious point of view and rules have also been laid down for the same.

The most famous book of economics is *Kautilya's Arthashastra.* It contains detailed instructions on religion, economics, politics, penal policy, etc. Apart from this, there are other important texts such as *Kamandakiy Nitisar*, *Nitivakyaamrita, Laghuarthniti* among others. Kautilya has described many types of devices, which were useful in war. The description of *Chakra Yantra*, *Sthiti Yantra,* etc. proves that the science of mechanics was developed in that age. Under aeronautics, everyone is familiar with the name *Pushpak Vimana.* The method of the creation of aircraft is described in the book *'Samarangana Sutra'*. In Bharadwaj's *'Yantra Sarvasva'*, there is a description of the construction of an aircraft.

There is a description of 360 bones in the human body in Vedic literature. In Sanskrit literature, insects have been classified on the basis of sound, structure of body, sex, effect of poison, wings, foot, mouth, hair, etc. According to Sushruta, there are six types of flies and ants. Other animals were also studied in the same way.

The tradition of studying botany dates back to the time of Rigveda. Plants were studied from the point of view of Ayurveda. In Sanskrit literature, trees have been described as living beings like humans.

Sushruta is still revered in the field of surgery. Maharishi Atreya was a scholar of Ayurveda. He wrote the *'Atreya Samhita'*. Atreya's disciples composed two texts. One describes *Kaya* therapy, which is known as *'Charaka Samhita'* today. The second book which is known as *'Sushruta Samhita'* describes surgery. In the Indian system of medicine, Dhanvantari is considered a god. The *'Sushruta Samhita'* was composed of his teachings. Sushruta's *'Sushruta Samhita'* describes nine hundred and twenty-five surgical instruments.

Panini's *Ashtadhyayi* and Patanjali's *Mahabhashya* are the best texts in the field of grammar. Panini is the best grammarian not only in India but in the entire world.

The mention of forensic science is found in the Vedic literature. Later, there is a deliberation on forensic science in Gautam Dharma Sutra, Baudhayana Dharma Sutra, Vashishta Dharma Sutra, etc. The mention of the Shrimad Bhagavad Gita is particularly noteworthy in this area. The entire Mahabharata is replete with principles of ethics.

Apart from these areas, important texts related to various other fields, such as music, literature, natural science, geography and astronomy, justice and logic, philosophy, social science, etc., were also composed by our ancient sages.

There are many other grounds for India to be called *Vishwa Guru*, such as-

- When science was not developed systematically, *Navagrahas* (nine planets) were worshiped in India.
- When the people of the West did not know how to wear clothes, India used to trade in silk clothes.
- When there were no means of travel like scooters, motorcycles, ships, etc., India had big airplanes.
- When there were no doctors, India had the knowledge of many medicines for easy recovery.
- India knew about the power of solar energy.
- There were great masters of Ayurveda like Charaka and Dhanvantari in India.
- When other countries used to have pieces of wood in the name of weapons, India had a huge stockpile of firearms, missiles, air weapons, and big nuclear weapons.
- Albert Einstein made discoveries regarding the atom only by researching our history.
- NASA is discovering planets in space only by researching our history.

- Asia and America are manufacturing big weapons by researching our history.
- Countries like Russia, Britain, America, Thailand, Indonesia, etc. are teaching Sanskrit in schools from childhood itself by researching our history.
- Based on the research of our history, the doctors are curing ailments like heart attack, BP, and major diseases of stomach, head, chest without injections, without medicines by asking people to simply chant *Omkar*. Big hospitals are being opened and given the names like *Omkar* therapy.
- Yoga was started in India by our ancient sages. Today, the whole world knows about the numerous benefits of yoga. That's why 21st June is celebrated as World Yoga Day. In today's era, meditation is an important way to get rid of various mental and physical problems.

I believe that India has an infinite ocean of knowledge, from which precious gems (inventions) can be obtained by diving (research), based on which India can lead the world. India can be re-established on the position of *Vishwa Guru* only on the basis of its Indianness.

Any country or society can carry out its all-around development - economic, religious, political, geographical, etc. - only when the teachers there are capable of becoming *gurus*. They should work not only to earn money but also for the upliftment of the country, society, and fellow human beings. May the bases of Indian culture contained in Indian literature - *'Vasudhaiva Kutumbakam'*, *'Sarve Bhavantu Sukhinah'* be imbued with the spirit of patriotism, which can inculcate love for the country and culture in the students and give them value-based cultured education.

For this, it is necessary that the curriculum of teachers' education should include the knowledge contained in ancient Indian literature. Only by doing this, a sense of pride, love, and dedication toward the country can be inculcated in the future teachers of the country.

❑

5.

Brahma Janati Bramhanah

(One becomes Brahman when one has known the Brahma, the ultimate and the supreme)

Having a dialogue with each other has been the core of our Indian culture. I personally believe that inter-faith dialogue is most important and relevant in today's times.

There are many misconceptions about the Brahmin community. I believe that Brahmins are not just a class but a highlight of Indian culture. In the history of social change in India, Brahmins have always taught lessons to humanity thereby giving positive direction to life. With the thought of the welfare of the country and the entire human race, the Brahmin community has carried out the important work of providing leadership to society. Who is a Brahman? Whenever I think about this, I can see visions of our Vedic Indian cultural traditions. It has been said in our country-

"Brahma janati bramhanah"

That means a brahman is one who knows Brahma. Brahman, that is one who knows about God. The ultimate truth of life is nothing else but God or the attainment of supreme knowledge. Therefore, it is the brahman who has carried out the work of making divine knowledge accessible for society, that is why Brahmins have always been the leaders in religion, culture, and education.

Since the tradition of the *Puranas*, the Brahman has been called a god. I have perused the scriptures a little. It has also been said that all the pilgrimages on the earth are found in the ocean and all the pilgrimages in the ocean are contained in the Brahman. He knows four *Vedas*. All the gods take shelter in his body.

The brahmin is good-natured and tolerant towards all- in mind, deed, and word. That is why it has been said –

"Brahman sarvejanasukhino bhavantu"

That means the brahmin is the one who wishes for the happiness and prosperity of all beings. That's why he is considered a god. It is believed that Brahmins are the children of *Saptarishis*.

The origin of Brahmins is considered to be older than the Vedic period. Therefore, Brahmins are also viewed on the basis of the four Vedas. For example, *Samavedis* were those who sang *Samaveda*. "*Agnihotris*" are those who recite the *Rigveda* that offers sacrifices in the fire. Dwivedi, Trivedi, Chaturvedi, etc. have also been associated with the knowledge of Vedas.

That is why the development of the culture of our country has been carried out incessantly by the Brahmins only. I also believe that Brahmin society has played a leading role in the making of modern India. The incessant contribution of Brahmins in literature, science, and technology, politics, culture, education, religion is immeasurable.

The Brahmin community which causes the current of culture to flow continuously is getting confused since the last few years. With the passage of time, malpractices and social evils are increasing in the community which has so far been free from depravity. When some people adopt social evils like dowry, superstition, drinking alcohol, the whole community gets defamed.

For one who calls himself a Brahmin, it is necessary that he should play his role in the development of society and nation while staying away from social evils and malpractices. They should avoid mutual jealousy, discord, and hatred. Then, this community will again be revered as the one that gives direction to the country.

Sometime back I read a very old article by Swami Sahajanand Saraswatiji about the Brahmin community. It was as if I learnt a lot of new things while reading him. From his writings, I learnt that there was even a separate text called *'Brahmanotpatti Martand'* written about the Brahmin community and that it contained many verses separately on Brahmins in the name of Puranas. The author of this book has concocted his own verses in the name of Puranas. There may be more such confusing texts. We should not be confused by such scriptures and their contents. Our culture has been 'Manurbhav', that is, it teaches us - 'Be human'. Brahmin is the one who teaches lessons in and of humanity.

Society is meant to move with the times. A society which lives in harmony with time, progresses and develops continuously. Sublime life values make a person great. Therefore, there is a need to contemplate more on how the energy of the Brahmin community and *Brahm* can be maintained in a man-made society. Certainly, towards this, we have to work for the nation and society with the spirit of sacrifice, while always thinking not only about our own welfare but also that of others. The Brahmin community has always worked for the welfare and well-being of humanity. Keeping this in mind, we have to create new paths for the future and keep others first.

❑

6.

Vedic Culture: God Given Constitution

Vedas are the first steps of knowing Indian knowledge and science. The entire Indian culture, art, literature, religion, science, and philosophy are inspired by Vedic principles and their spirit. At the beginning of any auspicious occasion, a few mantras of the Vedas are always recited. This is *mantra 'swasti-vachan'*. *'Swasti'* means one that causes good. There is a hymn in Rigveda –

"Aa no bhadraha kratavo yantu vishwatah"

That means, Oh Lord! May we receive good thoughts from all sides.

The meaning of the word 'Veda' is 'that which is eternal'; which is incomparably enlightened and in which there is a nectar store of hallowed thoughts. That's why I believe that if there is any book beneficial for the worldly and otherworldly, then it is 'Veda'.

Indian culture is called Vedic culture because the Vedas have given the ideals for all the actions related to life. At the beginning of the Vedas, 80 thousand mantras describe rituals. The Vedas describe sixteen types of rituals from conception to death. The Vedic vision and culture have been at the root of the development of the Saraswati Valley Civilization and Indus Valley Civilization.

Scholars from all over the world have appreciated this culture of ours by researching the knowledge contained in the Vedas. Leo Tolstoy is called the great humanist scholar, but he himself admitted in his writings that the hymns of the Vedas influenced him to the core and that they had an impact on him. The long tradition of German scholars like Schopenhauer, Heinrich Zimmer, etc. has been enriched and enhanced only by the study of Vedas.

It is said in the *'Bhoomi-Sukta'* of Atharvaveda, '*Bhoomi* (the earth) is my mother and I am her child'. Such expressions of respecting the nation as a mother and bowing down to it are found throughout the Vedas. That's why I also believe that the Vedas are oceans of knowledge imparting a sublime sense of nationalism. Therefore, all the people of the nation should adopt the teachings of the Vedas in practice which are imbued with the spirit of nationalism. That is why I consider the establishment of Veda Vidyapeeth to be very important.

I also believe that if parents rear their children according to the rituals described in the Vedas, then -all-around development of the child is bound to happen . I believe so because Vedas are the foundation of all the disciplines,

Puranas, history, and the scriptures like Ramayana, Geeta, Mahabharata, etc. All these were written only after the Vedas.

Our four Vedas i.e., Rigveda, Yajurveda, Samaveda, and Atharvaveda have been called the breath of God, that is, they have been created by God himself. The creation of the whole world is believed to have been originated in the Vedas. That is why they are also called *'Apaurusheya'* i.e., miraculous. According to *Manusmriti*, Vedas are *'Shruti,'* i.e., heard or perceived knowledge. From the beginning of creation till today, great sages have come to know the truth with the help of *Shruti Vedas*. The great knowledge acquired by the Vedic sages through *'samadhi'* and which was revealed for the welfare of the world is the Vedas.

There is no genre of life and literature, whose seed is not found in Vedic literature. That's why it has been said, *'Ananta Vai Vedah'*, that is, the Vedas are beginning-less, endless, and eternal and have been revealed by Brahma only for the benefit of the people.

Adi Shankaracharya had acquired the knowledge of all the *Vedas* and *Vedangas* at the age of eight and at the age of sixteen, he had written commentaries on all of them. When he turned 24, he defeated the anti-Veda brigade with his irrefutable arguments and raised the flag of Sanatan Dharma. He established *Vedic Dharma* in the entire world at the age of thirty-two and established four vast monasteries in all four directions.

The objective was that people should come out of their houses, explore the outside world and develop an inner understanding from the experience. So, he established pilgrimages in the form of monasteries in the four directions. It is from his early tradition of pilgrimage that today's tourism has been born.

Adi Shankaracharya made scientific establishments through Vedanta Sutras during his period. At the time when everyone was trying to project himself as great and a god, Shankaracharya said that the Vedas were supreme. He said that Vedas tell what God is, what are his characteristics, how he can be reached, etc. It is he who emphasised that the study of Vedas is necessary because if one does not read them, then anyone can mislead us by calling himself God. Think about it! What a unique vision he had!

The central thought of Vedic knowledge is the search for truth, light, and immortality. I also believe that Vedas are the constitution of God. There are many such mantras, learning from which human beings can attain the highest peak. In it is embedded the knowledge for making this world happy and the next world prosperous. The Vedas were called Shruti because of the rich Indian tradition of heard or perceived knowledge. Even after centuries of this tradition, the availability of this knowledge in this form today proves its authenticity and utility along with its perpetuity.

The knowledge of Vedas connects us to nature and environment through divine means and teaches us how to experience God in nature and how to establish harmony in life while preserving traditions along with modern development. There are dense forests in Banswara, Dungarpur, Pratapgarh districts of Rajasthan. There is also an abundance of tribal societies that follow nature worship. But it is also important that the knowledge of Vedas is indirectly preserved verbally in the tribal society even today in the form of nature worship and medicine.

I came to know some time ago that even today in the 'Nagar Brahmin' society in Banswara, there are self-singers of hymns of the *Shankhayan* branch of the Rigveda. I think that perhaps this tradition exists only in this place in the whole of India. *Veda-Vidyapeeths* (Vedic Universities) should be established to preserve the *Shankhayani* branch and revive the tradition of reciting the mantras of Samaveda. Only with this, we will be able to keep the glorious tradition of India intact. In addition to this,, we can also nurture the roots of the cultures of tribal societies. Govind Guru Tribal University in Bagad Kanthal has even taken initiative in this regard. But there is also a need that continuous efforts should be made at various levels to save the tribal culture of Vedas. Many languages have disappeared because they were not preserved. Similarly, it is also a concern that if the tradition of singing the mantras of Samaveda that has survived in the tribal areas is not conserved, then future generations will never forgive us. In this regard, initiatives should also be taken to preserve this tradition through digital media.

❑

7.

Bhagavad Gita Refines Life

I consider Shrimad Bhagavad Gita to be the essence of all scriptures. It is not just a scripture, rather it teaches the art of living life, following which one can live a meaningful life. Actually, Bhagavad Gita is the mantra of the skill of living life. Gita contains the inspiration for *Nishkaam Karma* (selfless action or action without any expectations or desire). If we delve into its verses and understand its greatness, then we will also come to know that the Gita not only contains knowledge about the conduct of life but it also teaches us to how to live life in a better way.

Lokmanya Bal Gangadhar Tilak had composed *'Gitarahasya'*. It is astonishing that he had written it down with a pencil in just five months. That was the period of British rule and every action of his was being monitored. He felt that the British government should not confiscate his writings. But he had great faith in his memory. He put together his experiences related to Gita in his mind and then wrote them down using his memory. Such is the Bhagavad Gita – if it is recited with sincerity, one does not need to memorize it. I have read Tilak's *'Gitarahasya'* and every time I read it, I feel like I am reading something new. This is the characteristic of good writing; it inspires you to read again and again.

The Bhagavad Gita has 18 chapters and 700 verses. In Indian culture, this holy book is included in *Prasthanatrayi*, i.e., it is included alongside Upanishads and Brahmasutras. That's why I also believe that the Bhagavadgita is not only a part of the Mahabharata but it is also a kind of summary of the Upanishads and Dharmasutras contained in the message of Lord Krishna. One who has not read the Upanishads and Dharmasutras but has read the Gita eventually understands the deep secrets of philosophy. The Brahmanism of the Vedas and the Spirituality of the Upanishads - both of these are inherent in the Gita.

In the Sanskrit literary tradition, such texts are called *Bhashya* (commentary) which are interpretable. In whatever way or manner the Gita is interpreted, it appears new every time. This is a commentary that not only has a micro vision of the teachings of Jnana Yoga, Buddhi Yoga, Karma Yoga, Bhakti Yoga, etc. but also has a wonderful hidden mantra to control the mind. There is such a beautiful euphemism in the Gita on how harmful anger is: an angry person gets confused and loses his sense of good and bad. So, when such a situation occurs, one should stay calm. Similarly, if the mind is disturbed, then the verses of the Gita inspire inner peace. I have always experienced it and motivate you to do it as well.

About the Gita, Mahatma Gandhi, the Father of the Nation said, "'I recall again and again.' Regarding his experiences related to Gita, he has said in 'Young India', "Whenever I am engulfed in the darkness of despair and hopelessness, become lonely and helpless and cannot see even a single ray of light, then I take refuge in Bhagavad Gita. I turn over the pages and recite various verses from different chapters and start smiling even during the moments of deep sorrow." I also feel that reciting the Gita frees the mind from the bonds of attachment.

In the Mahabharata, Lord Krishna narrated the Gita to Arjuna. This great commentary delivered during the Bhishma Parva of Mahabharata is a beautiful allegory of monotheism, Karmayoga, Jnanayoga, Bhaktiyoga. Every time you read it, you will feel like continue reading it. I cannot say exactly when I got attached to the Bhagavad Gita. It was probably due to my upbringing that I had started reciting the Gita in my childhood. I find the entire Gita like a beam of light through its verses. In the 50th verse of the 2nd chapter of the Gita, Lord Sri Krishna says – *'Yogah karmasu kaushalam'*, i.e., the skill or quality in action itself is yoga. This formula of management will not be found in any other religious text. From this perspective, the Gita is a way of cultivating life. There is a well-known verse of the Gita –

"Karmanyewadhikaraste ma faleshu kadachan
Ma karmfalheturbhurma te sangostwakarmani"

That means you have the right only to do the work and not reap its fruits. Therefore, O creature, do not act with expectations of the fruit nor should you think why do work without the expectation of results. Whenever this verse flashes in my mind, it is as if the way of life gets illuminated. I think if this verse is understood deeply, then this life can become easier and simpler. The great message to act neutrally and to consider your work itself as the reward is found only in the Gita and not in any other book in the world.

❑

8.

A Nation Narrating Cultural Tales of Valour and Power

For centuries, Rajasthan has been the land embodying immortal cultural consciousness, lauded for its immortal valour and unrivaled power. The famous English poet Kipling believed that if there is a place in the world where the bones of the heroes have transformed into the dust on the trail, then it is Rajasthan. This is the truth of our history. The tradition of sacrificing everything for the country continues even to this day in Rajasthan.

The Greater Rajasthan Union was formed on 30 March 1949 by merging the princely states of Jodhpur, Jaipur, Jaisalmer, and Bikaner. Since that day, it is celebrated as Rajasthan Day to mark the founding of Rajasthan. Rajasthan is not only the most widespread geographical state in India, but it is also one of the most beautiful ones. Its culture is well-known all over the world.

Various communities and rulers have contributed greatly to building the multidimensional culture of Rajasthan. As a result of this diversity, the moment Rajasthan is mentioned, we start visualizing huge palaces and forts, the Thar desert, camel rides, Ghoomar, Kalbelia dance, and colourful traditional costumes.

Along with valiant men, the heroic women also did not hesitate to make sacrifices for their land. History bears witness that the children of our land have made the name of Rajasthan shine like a star throughout the country and the world by performing wonderfully not only in the areas of bravery and courage but also in every other field. The bravest of hearts have been born in the land of Rajasthan. The fearless women have also contributed to the motherland with their sacrifices. Prithviraj Chauhan, who is called the brave warrior of the earth, was born here; he defeated Muhammad Ghori in the first battle of Tarain. It is said that Ghori had attacked Prithviraj 18 times and he had to face defeat 17 times. Prithvi, the 12-year-old son of Jaswant Singh, the king of Jodhpur, had torn the jaw of Aurangzeb's fierce hungry wild lion with his hands. Rana Sanga displayed courage by fighting more than a hundred wars. Along with the sacrifice of Panna Dhai, the sacrifice of Bagheli who was the queen of Thakur Mohkam Singh of Bulanda (Pali) is also immortal. In order to save Prince Ajit Singh of Jodhpur from Aurangzeb, she had secretly taken him away in the place of her newborn princess.

Rajasthan is famous all over the world for its pride, grandeur, valour, courage, sacrifice, and heroism. The people of Rajasthan are known to be hard working. Despite the geographical disparities and environmental challenges, the all-round development of the state has been possible due to the strong will and mutual cooperation of its citizens. The improvement in the social and economic conditions of the poor people of Rajasthan along with the growth in the resources and development in all the fields like politics, business, etc. is a symbol of our prosperity.

The people of Rajasthan are at the forefront of the country in all fields such as art-culture, tourism, trade, sports, and agriculture. Rajasthan is the largest state in the country. The area of the state is 3.42 lakh km. It is 10.41 percent of the total area of the country. The population of Rajasthan is 6.86 crore and the literacy rate is 66.1 percent. Rajasthan is made up of sandy, barren, mountainous, and fertile alluvial soil. At present, there are 7 divisions, 33 districts, 295 panchayat samitis, 9, 891 gram panchayats, 43, 264 inhabited villages, 184 urban bodies, and urban areas in Rajasthan. It has 200 Legislative Assembly constituencies and 25 Lok Sabha constituencies.

The economy of the state is based on agriculture and industries. Agriculture and animal husbandry are the main occupations of the people of Rajasthan. After independence, this state has definitely taken strides in progress and development. Due to the irregular rainfall, this region has been subjected to drought and famine many times, but the people of the state have learned to live in adverse conditions and maintain their high spirits.

we have indeed made progress in every field. The number of schools has increased. There has been a rise in the number of students enrolling. Food grains have become cheaper.. Electricity capacity has also increased. A large number of villages and houses are illuminated by electric lights. The network of roads can be seen everywhere. The villages are connected by main roads. Significant progress has been made in the field of drinking water. Water has reached to a number of villages. We now also have to keep moving forward diligently. The pace of development of Rajasthan has to be given continuous momentum.

Rajasthan is the centre of ancient artistic and cultural traditions. Its name implies - '*Raj Bhoomi*,' which means the land of truth, valour, and gallantry. It is the land of the bravery of Emperor Prithviraj Chauhan, Maharana Pratap, and Maharaja Surajmal. Devotees and seekers like Meera, Dhanna, Dadu, and Ramcharan-Ramsnehi have been the epitome of devotion in Rajasthan. Magha was the great Sanskrit poet from Bhinmal, while many scholars of Hindi and Rajasthani languages have also blessed this land.

Rajasthan has contributed to Indian art. Rajasthan has a literary tradition. Chandbardai's poem 'Prithviraj Raso' is noteworthy, whose earliest manuscripts date back to the 12th century. A popular medium of entertainment is the dance drama called *khayal* whose poetic themes are based on festivities, history, or romance. Rare antique items are found in abundance in Rajasthan, which includes Buddhist inscriptions, Jain temples, forts, magnificent princely palaces, mosques, and domes.

Rajasthan is the colourful land of fairs and festivals. There is a famous proverb in Rajasthan – '*Saat vaar, nau tyouhar*' i.e., seven days, nine festivals. The fairs and festivals here are indicative of the culture of the state. The cattle fairs held here show the interdependence of humans and animals. Among the state fairs, the Kartik fair of Pushkar, the fair of Tejaji of Parbatsar and Nagaur, and the fair of Kalyanji of Diggi are prominent. The festival of Teej is most important here. The series of festivals begins with this festival in the month of Shravan and continues till *Gangaur*. Hardly a month goes by in Rajasthan in which there is no religious festival. The most notable and special festival is *Gangaur*, in which clay idols of Mahadev and Parvati are worshiped by women. The procession of *Gangaur Mata*'s immersion is a sight to behold.

The biggest feature of Rajasthan is that both Hindus and Muslims participate in each other's festivals. These occasions are full of enthusiasm and gaiety. Pilgrims from India and abroad attend the Pushkar fair in search of salvation, while the shrine of Sufi spiritualist Khwaja Moinuddin Chishti in Ajmer is one of the holiest shrines in the world. On the occasion of Urs, lakhs of devotees from all over the country and abroad, arrive here to worship at the dargah. Hence, it would not be an exaggeration to call Rajasthan a major centre of festival tourism. Pushkar Fair is among the biggest attractions in the country. Every year lakhs of devotees come to Pushkar and take a dip in the holy lake.

Whether it is a native or a foreign tourist, Rajasthani culture captivates everyone instantly. After all, who would not like to see the beautiful Kalbelia dance? Nothing beats the Rajasthani costume where civilization and beauty blend. The traditional Rajasthani clothing for women is graceful, decent, graceful, and comfortable, while the *Bandhej* turban worn by men is unique.

In present-day Rajasthan, it is the responsibility of all of us to try and protect the *Sanatan* culture. Everyone should get a job. Every human being should be able to live with an identity of his own and self-respect. Every woman should be respected. When such an environment will be created, only then will there be a Rajasthan Day in the true sense. This time we have to move forward with new resolutions. The dreams of development in the state have to be realized. We have to be united keeping the interest of the country in mind. Rajasthan is a wonderful state of our country. The people here have preserved the Indian culture. The cities, towns, and villages here have different characteristics. Rajasthani folk songs touch the soul. The whole of Rajasthan seems to be symbolising Indian culture. The Marwari people here can play an important role in removing region-based inequality. Marwaris should come forward to strengthen their roots and contribute to the development of the region. Overseas Rajasthanis play an important role in making the economic system healthy.

A diverse state like Rajasthan with its hilly, desert, and

plain regions has been at the centre of the world due to its laboriousness, capability, beauty, morality, sacrifice, and strength. The purpose of celebrating Rajasthan Day is not limited to only describing the ancient history, rather, by keeping an eye on the current situation, we should discharge our duty in protecting Rajasthan. In recent times, the spirit of solidarity, patience, and mutual harmony displayed by the people of the state in preventing the spread of the corona virus is highly commendable and praiseworthy. The people of the state have taken a great initiative in making Rajasthan a healthy state by making concerted efforts to prevent coronavirus. I bow before the unity of the people of the state.

When the whole world is battling dreadful diseases like corona, our duty and responsibility become bigger and we should try our best to remedy the disorder. The land of Rajasthan is also not untouched by this pandemic. Some people in our state are also suffering from Corona. We have to defeat this epidemic with comprehensive work. Public awareness has to be spread and mutual understanding has to be increased. The people of Rajasthan have set an example by showing solidarity during the Corona crisis. After our call to help the people, the amount of Rs 21 crore deposited by the people in the Chief Minister's Relief Fund in a single day is highly commendable. This kind of unity and spirit of cooperation is definitely strengthening all of us and we all will be successful in defeating Corona.

❑

9.

Culture Engulfed in Sand Dunes

In December 2019, I had traveled to Jaisalmer, the border district of Rajasthan. At that time, I closely saw the diverse culture of the city settled on the sandbanks and the people living there with amazing vitality even in the harsh geographical conditions of the desert. I was quite thrilled to see the Sonar Fort built on a hill in Jaisalmer as well as the wood fossils that were crores of years old. I expressed in my writing my close experience of the Khaba village of Jaisalmer, the lakes built in the desert and the unique culture dwelling among the people. I wrote down in my diary whatever I saw during that time. Some excerpts from it are presented here.

Jaisalmer of Rajasthan is a wonderful city nestled in the sand dunes. The great feature of this city close to the Pakistan border is that it has a Sonar fort. This was the name given by Satyajit Ray to the Jaisalmer Fort. Satyajit Ray made 'Sonar

Kella' in 1974. Through this, in a way, he connected Bengal with Rajasthan. 'Sonar Kella' is the story of the reincarnation of a child Mukul who is haunted by memories of his past life in Rajasthan, the palace, the hidden treasure, war, and the golden fort. The house of Mukul - the protagonist of the story - shown in Jaisalmer and other scenes are remembered even today. After this, Sonar i.e., the fort of gold. This desert fort is a unique example of architecture on the mountain. But there are other attractions also in Jaisalmer. During my visit, I also saw the transformation that the trees and plants had undergone to take up the stone form millions of years ago. The Wood Fossil Park here is one of the world's most important geological phenomena. A lot of study and research has been carried out on these fossils in different parts of the world. Along with marking the sites of these fossils, museums and parks of fossils were also established in many countries of the world.

The Wood Fossil Park, established in the Akal of Jaisalmer district, can be called a wonder of the world. There are such parks in many other places in the world as well. However, this park which is located in Jaisalmer, the border and desert region of Rajasthan in the west of India, is famous for the oldest fossils. A large number of scientists and researchers from different countries of the world are always present here. When I read and resarched extensively about it, I also learnt that at some point in the past this whole region was a maritime zone. Later, it turned into a dry sandy desert. Today, the Jaisalmer district of western Rajasthan is the major centre of the oldest fossils and memorial fossils available.

Here, I saw a wonderful world of fossils from millions of years ago. Akal's Wood Fossil Park, located 18 km from the district headquarters on Barmer main road, is unique in the whole world. It is estimated to be 18 crore years old; there are fossils in America as well, which are considered to be 120 million years old. From this point of view, this fossil of Akal is probably the oldest in the world. Spread over an area of 108 hectares, the oldest wood fossils are preserved and displayed at various places in this sandy meadow and hilly park. About 180 million years ago, this entire region of western Rajasthan had a very humid warm climate, where there were dense forests with abundant tall trees.

During my visit to this park, I saw fossils of various shapes and sizes and realized that the trees had transformed into fossils. Later, due to geographical activities and frequent geographical changes, they again started appearing on the surface of the earth. Akal's Wood Fossil Park is also such an important site. Generally, as soon as the green flora and fauna die, they gradually decay until they are completely destroyed and their life ends. But in the second instance, if they get buried under the layer of soil at the bottom of an ocean a lake even before their development begins, then their erosion stops. Their hard parts like stem, seed, fruit, etc. gradually turn into stone. This gradual process takes centuries and their roots are transformed into organic and stony organic materials.

This process of transformation occurring at a slow pace is so condensed that even the microscopic cells that make up the tree are transformed into stone form. This process is called fossilization and the modified material is called a fossil. By studying these wood fossils scientifically, information about their age, vegetation of that time, climate and ecology, etc. is found.

Under the pressure of these layers, plant cells turn into silica and other mineral elements. The actual organic parts of the plant take the form of its basic elements and then the mineral elements present in different parts of the plant give different colours to its tissues. The effect of red, brown, and yellow in these wood fossils is visible because these fossils contain small amounts of various mineral elements, especially calcium and magnesium.

The region of Akal and the wood fossils found in it are an indication that the process of fossilization of dense forests started here 18 million years ago. It is also believed that at that time there was an abundance of non-flowering plants like pine, deodar, and red woods, etc. in this entire Bhrigu Bhirya region, which have been recorded according to monthly age. These trees were transformed into fossils in the standing position and after so many years of geographical changes are now visible on the sandy surface. Similar wood fossils are scattered all over the area.

The existence of fruits of that time has also been identified from the wood fossils available on the desert soil. This Wood Fossil Park in Akal has 18 wood fossils that are well present on the surface and are safely displayed. The tallest Wood Fossil is 13 meters tall and one meter in diameter. Many similar wood fossils are buried under the ground in this area. Similar wood fossils are also found in other areas of the Jaisalmer district. The entire area of Akal Wood Fossil Park is preserved as one of the oldest wonders of nature. For the first few years, it was under the Archaeological Survey of India, but in 1979, the Forest Department of the Government of Rajasthan took it under its jurisdiction. At present, this park is part of the Desert National Park operated under the Forest Department.

Akal Wood Fossil is famous as a museum of archaeological fossils in the country and the world. Many curious people and tourists keep coming here for research and study from all over the world. This park is open seven days a week. Its operational hours are as follows - From 1st March to 31st October - 8 am to 1 pm and 3 pm to 6 pm, and from 1st November to 28th February - 8 am to 1 pm and 2 pm to 5 pm.

Banner of Human Labour – Khaba

Jaisalmer is a border district of western Rajasthan. It has been a unique confluence of cultures. Being the centre of trade activities of various countries in the olden times, it was famous for both easy, safe, better trade routes and vibrant market. Due to the continuous movement of indigenous and foreign traders, many new cultures were incorporated in life here, due to which despite being a desert land, it remained the centre of rainbow traditions.

From the last two decades of the thirteenth century to the first two and a half decades of the nineteenth century, the Paliwal Brahmins dominated the folk life in the desert region. They established 84 villages in the Jaisalmer district with their hard work and dedication. Like Vishwakarma, these Paliwalas created a new world in the desert, in which all the amenities of ideal rural life were available. The availability and development of agriculture, trade, and animal husbandry also brought progress to these villages. For the people living in the desert, that period was no less than a golden age.

Khaba is a big village among these villages of Paliwals. Khaba, which is located 25 km from Jaisalmer district headquarter, is also one of the big villages that have been abandoned by the Paliwals. The settlements established by the Paliwals nine centuries ago in Khaba, which was a grand city and a major trading centre of its time, turned into ruins after being abandoned. Its remains spread over a large area reveal how advanced and prosperous it must have been. Hundreds of buildings that bear witness to human labour still evoke memories of the bygone era. Visible from miles away, Khaba Fort situated on the hill is a centre of attraction for domestic as well as foreign tourists. Tourists enjoying camel safari and sunny evenings on the velvet sandy beaches enjoy glimpses of Kuldhara and Khaba.

Like Kuldhara, Khaba village was an internationally famous trading market of that time. This village was established by Harlal Gautri Paliwal Brahmin. During the golden age of the Paliwals, traders from many countries used to gather in Khaba. During those days, all the Paliwals used to gather in Khaba fort on the day of the Dussehra festival which was celebrated on a huge scale. Near the fort is the ancient temple of *Mahishasura*, which is a place of reverence.

The fort of Khaba exhibits not only the architecture of the ancient palaces but also the ancient civilization and culture. Khaba fort has become a centre of curiosity and attraction for tourists after it got a new look post renovation. A multidimensional collection is displayed in various parts of the Khaba fort.

There is a cultural museum in one part of the fort, in which the tableau of the ancient Paliwal civilization and culture is displayed. It contains items that were useful in daily life during that era, such as various tools, utensils, etc., which have a very different artistic designs. Apart from these, the everyday life of people and Paliwal history has been displayed in this museum where beautiful photos have been included. From the ruins of Khaba Fort and its museum and far-flung settlements, the then urban and rural splendour and comfortable life can be easily imagined.

The city that treasures the unique beauty of Sonar Fort

Sonar Fort is a major attraction of Jaisalmer. This fort looks like a ship anchored on a hill and looks so attractive from afar that one feels like keep looking at this fort which is situated in the middle of the desert. This fort, nestled among the wonderful and unique gifts of nature, natural beauty, and picturesque geographical location, is a unique heritage of India. That is probably why UNESCO has included it in the World Heritage.

I remember reading somewhere that Lata Mangeshkar had once called it a 'rose of sand'. Lata is a nightingale of music; it is natural that as soon as she felt the music in the sand dunes, she called the stone art a 'rose of sand'. I saw it and I just could not take my eyes off it.

With the gradual development of human civilization, the new world was created by civilizations and cultures from all over the world which has human labour and imagination in living forms. In the past centuries, , cities, forts, palaces, and temples established in India were full of architectural wonders. Those wonders cannot be seen anywhere else in the world. Even after centuries, these ancient heritage sites remain the centre of attraction for researchers and philosophers all over the world.

The glory of the world-famous Sonar fort, located in the middle of the desert spread on the western outskirts of Rajasthan, is also unique in that it is a unique example of the art-culture, valour, and bravery of western Rajasthan. Sonar fort gives a glimpse of history, divine energies, spirituality, every aspect of the speciality of desert life, and golden images of the surroundings. Sonar Fort has been the centre of attraction for centuries not only for India but also for the world. That's why even after traveling thousands of miles across the seas, people experience comfort when they find themselves in the valleys of Jaisalmer.

At the beginning of the twentieth century, Jaisalmer was famous on the global trade map as a major trading marketplace. This was the easy and accessible desert route for import-export and trade of valuable goods from Afghanistan, Sindh, Iran, Iraq, China, Russia, and European countries, where camels were traded. The fort of Jaisalmer has been a witness to and centre for the trade of diamonds and jewels, perfumes, gold, and other valuables. This area, which was the center of indigenous and foreign civilizations, cultures, tales of bravery, and human movement, kept the golden age alive. As a result of these singularities, the river of freshness, beauty, and gaiety in Jaisalmer has been flowing unceasingly in every era. From time immemorial, Jaisalmer has been a symbol of the golden island shining in the ocean of sand.

The magnificent fort situated on the Trikuta mountain has an amazing ability to attract tourists. Anyone who hears about it develops a wish to visit it. Even today, Sonar fort remains busy welcoming domestic and foreign tourists throughout the year. Situated on the Trikutas mountain, the Sonar fort is made of yellow stones, the yellow sun rays falling on it illuminate it with a golden aura and from a distance, giving an impression of a golden fort. Situated on the Trikuta mountain, the Sonar fort is also made of yellow stones. That is why it was named 'Sonar Fort'.

Many TV serials, documentaries, and films from Bollywood, Hollywood, etc. have exalted Sonar Fort. Jaisalmer has also been associated with mythological stories and myths. It is a popular belief that Lord Krishna and the Pandavas have blessed the desert by walking on its soil. According to legends, after the Mahabharata war, while visiting Valla Mandal they saw the sage Uttanga undergoing severe penance on Trikuta mountain, stayed in his ashram, and granted the boon as per the wish of the sage that there will come a time when the thirst of this craving earth will be quenched. Today, the Indira Gandhi Canal is a reality and a boon. According to another legend, during the journey from Dwarka to Hastinapur, Shri Krishna and Arjuna stayed here for rest. At that time, regarding the future of this region, Krishna had told Arjuna that this land had a deep relationship with the *Yaduvanshis* and that in *Kaliyuga* only a *Yaduvanshi* king would build a fort on this hill and establish his capital.

At that time, when Arjuna was thirsty, Lord Krishna had revealed the eternal source of sweet water by digging wells on the Trikuta mountain with the help of Sudarshan Chakra. In some places, it has been said that Arjuna had also dug a well with an arrow. These wells are famous by the name 'Jaislu wells'.

Centuries after the end of the Krishna era a *Yaduvanshi* king named Jaisal considered his capital in the desert unsafe and decided to build an impregnable fort at a safe location in Jaisalmer and started looking for a place for it. There was an *Aksahvani* (oracle) and the king got a signal. He arrived at this hill which was 10 miles east of Lodrava with a royal priest and learned Brahmins, where the transmuting ascetic hermit Baba Isaal was meditating in his hut. Jaisal prostrated in front of him. Acharya Baba Isaal welcomed the king and resolving his curiosity told him that Trikuta mountain was a perfect place for building a fort.

Baba Isal told him about Lord Shri Krishna staying on this hill and setting up a well during *Dwapar Yuga* and taking him near the well showed him the prophetic inscription engraved there. Its meaning is that a *Yaduvanshi* king named Jaisal will build a new fort here and establish his capital on this mountain. These surprising developments astonished Jaisal. Baba Isaal also told Jaisal about the future signs. He said that this fort will create a history of valour and heroism. It will collapse two and a half times. Rivers of blood will flow and the flames of heroic women's pyres will burn bright. For a short time, it would be subjugated by others, but later it would become known throughout the world. Jaisal began the construction of the fort on the Trikoot mountain on the day of *Shravan Shukla Dwadashi* in *Vikram Samvat* 2012. He named it Jaisalmer by combining Jaisal and Meru. This same Jaisalmer is at the height of fame in the country and the world today.

The War Museum is also located here. It is well organized. The concept of this museum, which outlines the history of the Indian Army, is historical. Our future generations will be able to know the history of national defense through this glorious heritage. I bow to the brave martyrs who laid down their lives defending the nation. The nation is paramount. I salute the soldiers of the Indian Army deployed on the border for maintaining the unity, integrity, and security of India. The Indian Army has made robust arrangements for the security of the country. I spoke to soldiers to learn about their military experience. The soldiers spoke about their military experience, tank operation, and various technical aspects. They also introduced me to various military equipment, including the Arjun tank, which showed might on various fronts. They also shared information about the special aspects of their experiences related to their operation. ❑

THE CULTURE OF EDUCATION

10.

New Education Policy and India

Educational institutions are not identified by their beautiful buildings and facilities but by their contemplative tradition. The measure of the competence of education is nurturing humans imbued with the values of Indian culture. The meaning of teacher is that such examples should be set among the students by our conduct, from which the students can learn about the values.

Education aims to shape the individual. Therefore, it should not remain formal, rather it should also be concerned with the formation of personality. This develops the power of critical and opinionated thinking in the students.

The new education policy of the central government has been prepared after consultations with 676 districts, 6600 development blocks, 2.50 lakh gram panchayats, teachers, and common people across the country. This is probably the first such education policy after independence, in which the participation of people has been ensured on such a large scale. It is also important that it has a flexible approach allowing exploration of vocational and non-vocational subjects along with co-curricular and extra-curricular activities.

I believe that the new education policy, which has come after 34 years, is going to nurture the ideology of nationalism among the students as well as decide the important role of the students in the long-term development of the country. It will completely meet the notions, aspirations, and expectations of the Indian public. Under the policy, the plan of encouraging education in mother tongue/s, on which universities need to take practical action is also discussed.

An important aspect of this new education policy is that it has given freedom for study related to the sacraments associated with Indian philosophy along with science, art, culture. I believe that the student's own interest in the subject of education is very important. If he is interested and passionate about what he is studying, only then he can grow academically over time.

I have studied the new education policy in detail and feel that it is completely student-centric. It clearly states that neither any language will be imposed on the student nor any language will be opposed. I consider it very important to study in the mother tongue because it will actually help in preserving and promoting Indian languages. We all know that the child can get a better education in the language in which he communicates with his parents at home. It is also important because it keeps the student practically connected to his environment, and the education that he acquires later proves useful to him throughout his life. Today, when work is being done with a focus on all-round development, then it is necessary that the universities should develop courses in science and technology and also in the areas of specialized knowledge in Hindi along with English. Educational institutions should make efforts to bring research and studies related to local knowledge and science in as many mother tongues as possible. With this, we will be able to preserve the heritage of knowledge available along with our tradition and culture in a better way for the future as well. The main objective of the new education policy is also to preserve our heritage in the interest of the students.

The new education policy also lays special emphasis on enhancing the understanding of Indian art and cultural heritage. In this, the issue of independence for the students to choose the subjects is also very important. Earlier students could not study the subjects of their choice and there was pressure on them to study other subjects. But now under the new education policy, as students will study their favourite subjects, they will not only develop self-confidence but they will also be able to do something better for the society in future taking their own interests forward.

Universities and higher educational institutions should invite subject experts related to art, literature, and culture as guest lecturers and introduce them to the students. To make the regular curriculum interesting, dimensions related to art, literature, and culture should be added to it. In this way, education will become meaningful for wider purposes. Comprehending the purpose of the new education policy, universities should develop e-courses in regional languages according to the demand of modern times. They should develop virtual labs and ensure their participation in a national educational technology forum right now.

A country becomes future-ready with education. Naturally, for this, education should get a major share of GDP. That is why the target of investing six percent of the country's GDP in education has been set in this policy. Qualitative growth in the level of research in higher education is also necessary. The new education policy envisages the establishment of the National Research Foundation (NRF) as an apex body for a robust research culture. The main objective of the NRF would be to enable a culture of research through universities. For the first time in the country, such a provision has been made in the education policy for the development of research culture independently. Universities should develop such a culture of latest research and studies that the students are encouraged to make original contributions based on their own experience. They should be encouraged to take time in their research and gather all information they can from various resources rather than just mugging everything up from a single reference.

❑

11.

Technical Education based on Human Values

Education is that cultural process in which new trends of action and thought are always developing. Education is a cultural process. This means that there is a continuous development of such methods in education which bring about a continuous positive change in the life and conditions of man. Technology may be predominant in technical education, but it has to be understood deeply that the training of technology should be based on humanity.

It is said in our country – *'Sa vidya ya vimuktaye'*, that is, that is, education frees a person from all those dogmas, which block the development of humanity. It is natural since technology is the means, not the end. Basically, technical education aims to do good for society using technology.

There is a well-known mantra from Rigveda – *'Aa no*

bhadra kratavo yantu vishwatah' that is, wherever and whatever is good, beneficial to humanity, should come to us from all directions. That's right, technical knowledge has given us a lot in physical terms. The use of machines has opened the doors of unlimited possibilities in life. But it has also led to neglect of human values, traditions, and ideals on many levels.

With the knowledge and teaching of technology alone, people tend to become biased and insensitive. Therefore, the inclusion of human values in technical education is very important. If this is taken care of in technical educational institutions, then only we can sustain while prospering technically and culturally.

Swami Vivekananda had called education the mantra of the development of life. He believed that obtaining information, learning from books, or making one mechanical by forcibly restricting desires is not education. Education is that which builds human life and character, develops the will, and makes one realize the divinity inherent in himself.

The development of infinite energy, boundless enthusiasm, and unlimited patience should be the aim of education. What Swamiji has said has deep inference in technical education and teaching. Personally, I believe that technical knowledge and research in technical education are not related to bookish knowledge. There is a need to pay more attention to how the student transfuses some of the technical knowledge, that he acquires in educational institutions in his thinking. Technological knowledge gives a new perspective on life. This education expands the horizon of the student. Education unveils the secret of knowledge in life and in a way, frees one from ignorance giving him the means to live a quality life.

If education based on human values is included in technical education, then we can save the students from the aimlessness prevailing in them on a large scale. We can prevent them from being inertial in the teaching and training of mechanical knowledge. If human values are included in technical education, then a student will have the self-confidence, he needs to face the outside world. After completing his education, he would not be afraid but ready to accept the world with open arms. He will be confident enough to make something out of life using his knowledge and skills and also use it ,for the welfare of entire humanity.

By doing so, we will not only be able to save the student from being mechanical, but we will also be able to see his knowledge being used in our farms and barns, in the factories of our country, in different aspects of the self-reliant economy. This is a period when the whole world is going through an economic crisis due to the Corona epidemic. In this context, an important initiative has been taken in India in the form of the package of 'Self-reliant India'.

Our technical educational institutions need to think seriously about how we can develop the technical skills and knowledge to be applied there as an opportunity for the economy. Something meaningful can be achieved in this direction only through human value-oriented education.

Education of human values means that moral, social, cultural, and spiritual values should be included in it. In this, emphasis should be laid on inculcating values in various subjects in a psychological manner and incorporating them into the overall personality of the students.

Madan Mohan Malaviyaji used to tell a message of three words which is enough for the students – power, power, and power. First is physical power, the second is mental power and the third is spiritual power. There is a need to integrate this message into technical education. We should not forget that our ancient knowledge or science has been very rich along with being the conductor of human values. Sage Kanad has described light and heat as different forms of the same element in physics.

In the oldest well-known texts of chemistry, *'Rasratnakar'* composed by Nagarjuna occupies a prominent place. Adi Shankaracharya's *guru* Sri Govind Bhagavatpad wrote an important book called *'Rasahrudaytantra'*. Apart from this, our precious heritage of ancient Indian texts of chemistry includes *'Rasendrachudamani'*, *'Rasaprakash Sudhakar'*, *'Rasarnav'*, *'Rassar'* etc. Aryabhatta showed the path of independent development of Indian algebra. Kautilya's economics is valid all over the world even today. In ancient Sanskrit texts related to technology, *'Kashyapa Shilpa'* and in ancient mining-related texts *'Ratnapariksha Loharnav'*, *'Dhatukalpa'*, *'Lohapradip'*, *'Pashanvichar'* etc. have shown a way to modern technological knowledge at many levels. The purpose of all this is that our advanced tradition of technology has always been associated with human welfare. We cannot lay a strong foundation for the future if we forget tradition. Therefore, it is also necessary that the students should always stay connected with the values of traditional knowledge.

If we incorporate our ancient tradition in technical education along with human values, then the students will have more thriving character and morals. Technical education makes the student capable. If human values are included, then the thinking of the person receiving this education expands.

Instead of being self-centered and using the knowledge gained only for himself, he is motivated to use the knowledge he has acquired for the universal welfare. Only through human values, technical education can be a vehicle of human welfare in the true sense. With this, we can truly realize the idea of *'Vasudhaiv Kutumbakam'* i.e., the whole world is one family. This is also the main aim of our culture.

❑

12.

Education with Information and Communication Technology

India is a young nation. 60 percent of the population in India is below 30 years of age, which is directly or indirectly connected with higher education. Therefore, higher educational institutions are expected to instill in the youth loyalty to God, faith in the present, and hope for the future. The COVID-19 pandemic has further reinforced the challenge of shaping the future of this youth in higher educational institutions in India.

Today the entire humanity is fighting for its existence against Covid-19. The challenges in higher education institutions have become bigger than ever in this time of calamity as they have in other aspects of life. Students, parents, and academics around the world are feeling the effects of the extraordinary wave of the deadly corona virus. This epidemic has not only disrupted the teaching process across all schools and colleges, but it has also opened new avenues in the field of education.

Distance learning has emerged as a major medium in education. Through this, every effort is being made to provide quality education to all the stakeholders during this time. During the third week of March, the threat of Corona led to disruption in the face-to-face classroom teaching system in all colleges and universities in India. For most of the higher educational institutions with the traditional annual examination system, it was time for an annual examination, and semester exams in colleges with a semester system.

With everything in absolute middle, it was very difficult to shift the education system in universities suddenly to online mode. However by ensuring its delivery at all levels, a message was also sent out that if there is a will, there is bound to be a way for education. I believe that the strength of any institution lies in the faculty. In today's changing environment, there is a need for the faculty to change their traditional teaching methods and develop technology-centric teaching methods.

The faculty should establish themselves as 'competent' individuals, who can meet the expectations of the students. A multi-pronged strategy is needed to manage the crisis and build a resilient Indian education system in the long run. Along with this, it is also the need of the hour for higher educational institutions to implement immediate measures to ensure continuity of teaching in colleges and universities.

Open-source digital learning solutions and learning management software should be adopted to enable teachers to conduct online learning. Inclusive learning solutions, especially for the most vulnerable and marginalized sections, need to be developed. With the rapid growth of mobile internet users in India, technology is enabling universal access and personalization of education even in the remotest parts of the country.

In order to make the curriculum accessible to the weakest students, education needs to be reachable even to the students in remote areas using both online and offline teaching methods. Better use of technology will also have to be considered to provide quality education to the students in remote areas of the country. It can transform our education system and increase the effectiveness of learning and teaching, giving students and teachers many options to choose from.

The evolving demand-supply trends around the world will require specific strategies to prepare the higher education sector, particularly related to the global mobility of students and faculty along with improving the quality and demand for higher studies in India. In addition, urgent measures will be needed to reduce the impact of the pandemic on planning proposals, internship programmes, and research projects.

With regard to conducting examinations and evaluations of the answer sheets, it is also important to consider how work can be done at a fast pace and what kind of technology should be used. It is also important to rethink the current transition to higher education and the educational system. It is also necessary to seamlessly integrate classroom teaching with e-learning mode to build an integrated learning system. The major challenge in technical education reforms at the state level is the seamless integration of technology into the current Indian education system, which is one of the largest in the world.

Apart from this, it is also important to establish quality assurance mechanisms and quality standards for online learning, developed by higher education institutions across the nation. Today, different universities and institutions offer the same content in the curriculum in different formats with different certification, methodology, and evaluation parameters at different levels.

In the COVID-generated scenario, we have to conduct this teaching method as we discuss the implementation of an e-learning system. For e-learning, we will need another platform along with the Internet, which is comprehensive and can fulfill the need of many more students at any time.

A timetable should be made, in which the theory periods should be conducted through distance and e-learning in the initial two or three months. Thereafter, the students may be called to the campus in small groups as needed for practical experiments in laboratories and practical experiences in the field. If necessary, the balance of theoretical and practical components can be redefined by making necessary changes in the curriculum. For this, active brainstorming will be required at the faculty level.

Fortunately, technology has provided us with many new dimensions and techniques for teaching, which are extremely relevant in the current situation. Technologies like Augmented Reality (AR) and Virtual Reality (VR) can make learning interactive and engaging. Applications of virtual reality can be included in practical learning, in which mixed reality is included.

The crisis caused by COVID-19 is an opportunity to change the higher education system. Institutions and universities should use this opportunity to transform themselves. They should focus on promoting online learning systems in higher education, curriculum restructuring to find the right balance of theoretical as well as practical components, collaboration, skill development, and active faculty participation.

There is also a need to use effective methods in education to efficiently face all the obstacles to achieve the best in the present circumstances. Education becomes meaningful only when it moves with time. For this, it is also necessary to impart effective training in online mediums related to the latest technology of means of communication in education at the faculty level. This will make online learning more consistent in the future.

❑

13.

Higher Education in Sync with Times

Along with strengthening the higher education system in the country, it is also required that higher education should give students' future a positive direction in a practical way. In the light of the new education policy in the country, the development of higher education needs to be seen from this perspective. This is because the new education policy, which was introduced in the country after 34 years, along with nurturing the ideology of nationalism in the students, is going to decide the important role of teachers and students in the long-term development of the country. I believe that it fully meets the notions, aspirations, and expectations of the Indian public.

In addition to education, vocational education, and its effective implementation, will also have a completely new perspective on teacher's education.

Our scriptures have a phrase - *'Neti-Neti'*, which means 'there is no end'. Everything that is going on is not the truth. We still have a long way to go. The new education policy also needs to be seen in this context. There is no limit to knowledge and I consider universities to be an inexhaustible source of knowledge. I believe that universities are the lighthouses that illuminate the whole society. Along with nurturing our ancient traditions of knowledge, the new education policy is also motivating new paths of modern knowledge. In the new education policy, freedom has been given for studies related to science, art, culture as well as teachings associated with Indian ideology.

The student's own interest in education is very important. Only through this, his all-around development is possible over a period of time. From this standpoint, the new education policy is completely -student-centric. It clearly states that neither any language will be imposed on the student nor any language will be opposed. 'Subsection 15.4' of this policy lays special emphasis on the high standard of quality along with a variety of methods of teaching the subjects being taught to students. Similarly, special attention has also been given to raising the capacity of teachers. Under this, there is a discussion about connecting teachers with the highest level in society, along with other high-level professionals. The aim is that there should be qualitative development of higher education in the country promoting it to the global level. I also believe that reverence for the teachers should be paramount.

Maharishi Arvind had once said that the teacher is the gardener who beautifies the nursery called society by weeding and hoeing it. Therefore, revering the teacher is equal to honoring the nation. It is the teachers who undertake the greatest mission of character building for the future generation of the country. So, respecting them means working to make our future better.

In the new National Education Policy, special attention has been paid to the training and capacity building of teachers. I believe that in this era of information and communication technology, teachers associated with higher education have lot many responsibilities. They not only have to teach in the classroom, but they also have to disseminate the latest knowledge among the students by making better use of the means related to high technology. Naturally, for this, there is a need to focus more on increasing the efficiency of teachers through better training.

Effective implementation of vocational education and through this the idea of 'Self-reliant India' can be realized in the true sense only when the universities work to prepare teachers through an excellent system of training keeping up with times. There is a special emphasis on this in the new education policy.

Universities and their affiliated colleges should become centres of research and knowledge. Educational institutions should not be identified by their beautiful building and facilities but by their tradition of contemplation. The measure of the competence of education is the nurturing of human beings imbued with the values of Indian culture.

I consider education to be a three-pronged process. The important links in this process are the teacher, the student, and the curriculum. The noble function of the teacher is to teach the learner and the curriculum is the medium. The basic purpose of education is to make all three dimensions-intellect, mind, and body of a human being healthy and make him civilized, cultured, and development-oriented. Universities should enable students to enter through the new doors of ever-increasing modern research and knowledge opening up in the world.

On this occasion, I am especially reminded of Gurudev Rabindranath Tagore and his contemplation related to the Shanti Niketan established by him. Gurudev had once said, "If the teacher does not study himself, he cannot impart true education. How can an extinguished lamp light another lamp? If a teacher has stopped studying his subject, has stopped developing his knowledge further, and keeps on repeating the same things, does not do justice to the students. He cannot sharpen their minds. Therefore, the teacher should remain a lifelong student."

Today, when information is spreading rapidly and every day new inventions are taking place in the fields of knowledge and science around the world, it is necessary for universities to develop such a teaching-learning system that students along with the static curriculum-based knowledge, also remain updated with the latest knowledge and science. Students should not engage in rote learning alone. Rather their minds should be prepared in such a way that they can take on the mantle of major decision-makers of positive change in society in the future by participating in all kinds of information in their surrounding environment.

We have had a glorious ancient tradition of imparting education in our country. The mobile University of Maharishi Durvasa usually had almost ten thousand students. Valmiki, Vashistha, Angira, Bharadwaj, etc. were the ancient Vice Chancellors. Sage Sandipani was the guru of Lord Krishna and Sudama. They imparted education in conducting life in which human welfare was implicit.

Accepting the challenges arising in education with the changing times, educational institutions must develop the system of learning and teaching in such a way that not only can the excellent training of teachers be implemented effectively, but also professional and qualified students can be trained in various faculties according to the needs of the country.

Comprehending the aim of the new education policy, universities should develop curricula according to the demands of modern times, which will not only ensure the employment of the students themselves but will also enable them to employ others.

The future of a country is equipped with education. Naturally, for this, education should have a major share of GDP. In the new education policy, the target of investing six percent of the country's GDP in education has been set so that through education not only can we effectively implement the idea of a 'self-reliant' India, but also make India the *Vishwa Guru* (World Teacher) again.

Efforts to update the courses which have been continuing for years in universities are also the need of the hour. It should also be seen whether the theoretical books of physics, chemistry, economics, etc. which have been continuing for many years are still useful. Considering their usefulness in the context of modern times and their requirements in the light of the latest knowledge, action should also be taken to implement their revised and latest versions. Similarly, the syllabi which have not been updated for a long time should also be updated in line with the aim of the new education policy.

I categorically believe that the aim of education should not be to create bookworms. The education that is disseminated in the universities should be such that it not only prepares responsible citizens of the country but also students who will strive together for the prosperity of the country.

❑

CULTURE IN THE LIGHT OF PEOPLE

14.

Mahatma Gandhi: Light in the Path of Life

The life of Mahatma Gandhi has been a message of inspiration not only to India but to the whole world and the entire humanity. From the very beginning, I have believed that his life and his work have given him such a stature that even today, 150 years after his birth, not only we are getting inspiration, but they also have messages for future generations. Gandhiji spent very little time of his life in independent India. Despite this, we see that today the development and concept of development of the country are incomplete without his principles like *Swadeshi Gram Swarajya* and *Swavalamban.*

Mahatma Gandhi was a personality whose principles, rising above elements like country, religion, language, caste, sect, and class would remain useful and relevant to the entire humanity. If we look at history, Gandhi's impression is visible in all the movements against imperialism across the world during the last century.

Whether Nelson Mandela in South Africa or Martin Luther King in America, Yasser Arafat in Palestine, or Lech Walesa in Poland, all of them considered Gandhi as their inspiration in some way or the other. Gandhiji's thoughts and conduct as well as his unwavering devotion to his principles and non-violence changed the direction of movements in many countries around the world.

Satyagraha - the path provided by Mahatma Gandhi emerged as a major medium for expressing dissent and protest around the world. Gandhiji showed that it was possible to protest by adopting a non-violent way and that a great power like Britain could be made to retreat from not only India but many other countries.

The way to solve the big challenges faced by the world today also opens up through Gandhiji's thoughts. The whole world is facing the challenges of environmental imbalance, terrorism, character degradation, and indiscriminate development. Mahatma Gandhi very briefly described a simple way of shaping men, society, and nation.

A list of seven social sins enumerated by Gandhiji was published in the October 22, 1925 issue of 'Young India' newspaper. He mentioned these 7 sins that should be avoided - politics without principle, wealth without deeds, happiness without soul, wealth without character, business without morality, science without humanity, and worship without sacrifice.

According to Gandhi, ethics, economics, politics, and religion are separate units; however, the purpose of all these is the same that is *Sarvodaya* (Upliftment of all). Politics cannot be pure if it is aimless and not based on ideals. Similarly, money earned without hard work and by unfair means can be called stolen money. When Gandhiji talked about the soul, he referred to that inner voice that makes one aware of right and wrong. Similarly, science that works against humanity is not a blessing but a curse.

Mahatma Gandhi not only emphasized the need for the people working in the public sector to have a moral character, but himself lived his whole life setting an example of sacrifice. Non-violence is the mantra given by Gandhiji, in which lies the latent possibilities of world peace. He had said that non-violence is not for cowardly people. Lord Mahavir Swami also said the same thing thousands of years ago - *'kshama veerasya bhushanam'*. Today, it is time to recognize the power of non-violence.

Mahatma Gandhi's path of *Gram Swarajya, Swadeshi,* and *Swavalamban* is particularly worth adopting. Self-reliance is a philosophy of life that prevents man from becoming dependent on others. As a result of this, the nation is filled with self-disciplined individuals and communities who understand the importance of labour and are not afraid to strive hard for their sustenance.

India was always a country that was satisfied despite its deprivations. The villages here were totally self-sufficient. In the 18th and 19th centuries, colonialist forces plundered the resources of prosperous India. Gandhiji recognized the strength of the soul of India, the unwavering faith of the citizens in religion, and the disposition of the country to be non-dependent. He turned what was considered a weakness into a strength.

Gandhiji had given an amulet, which I would like to

mention in particular. Gandhiji said - I will give you a talisman. Use it whenever you are in a dilemma or when your selfishness overwhelms you. Remember the face of the poorest and weakest person you have ever seen and ask yourself – will the step that I am going to take be of any use to that poor person? Will he be benefitted from this step? In other words, will this step give autonomy to lakhs of hungry and spiritually poor people? Then you will find that all your doubts and selfishness have melted away. This talisman is likewise effective even today.

Our country is a confluence of different religions, castes, languages, and cultures. This diverse culture makes India unique in the whole world. Now is the time to maintain and preserve this culture. Poverty, illiteracy, and social backwardness are prominent among the challenges facing the country. The government is working continuously for the overall development of the citizens of the country. The cooperation of all the people is very necessary to maintain the momentum of these activities. Cooperation and peaceful existence are also an integral part of our culture.

This is the time when it is the responsibility of every one of us to take the country on that path where all the people can keep faith in their respective beliefs and experience freedom. Mahatma Gandhi's thoughts and his life can prove to be most useful in this task. From the elementary classes itself, the students must be taught about the life and work of our national heroes. Along with this, students should also be taught how to imbibe those principles in practical life.

Mahatma Gandhi's thoughts remain relevant even today. His principle of trusteeship is so inspiring that all development goals can be achieved by following them.

He had said that those who are in the government should not consider the property of the public as their own. Instead, they should consider it as that of the entire community and act as its trustee. This will set an example of honesty and morality.

Today, the whole world is concerned about the damage being caused to the environment. In this regard, the path laid down by Mahatma Gandhi can be walked upon. He emphsised that goods and services should be produced in-house. Every household should produce the needed goods using the resources available to them. This can eliminate the problem of pollution and environmental imbalance. In this direction, the government has started an important effort to make India free from single-use plastic. I urge you all to participate in this movement. This will solve a lot of problems that may occur in the future.

The government has also sent out a message through *Swachh Bharat Abhiyan* (Mission Clean Indian), which has yielded meaningful results. Participation by all sections of the society in this campaign is encouraging. Water conservation is our priority today. The need of the hour is to tackle the water crisis and preserve the birthright to water for our generations.

If we read Mahatma Gandhi in detail, then we will also learn that whatever problems we are facing today, he had given the solutions for them continuously during his time as well through his thoughts. He is also relevant because he has shown us the light of life while understanding the pulse of the time.

❑

15.

From Cultural Nationalism to the Path of Non-Violence

We all address Mahatma Gandhi as 'Father of the Nation'. Whenever I ponder about this title, his ideals associated with the nation and his sublime vision of taking everyone along starts flashing in my mind. I believe that it was Gandhi who gave a comprehensive outlook on the freedom movement and linked it with Indian culture and values.

The development of our country as a nation is not only due to the existence of the land or any political power but because of our culture which is more than five thousand years old.

The development of our country as a nation has not taken place only because of its land and existence of any political power but also because of our culture which is more than five thousand years old. In spite of diversity in languages and regional traditions over a large area, the values of our culture have remained alive. Gandhiji linked this very cultural vitality with the values of non-violence and moral life during the freedom movement. This was his cultural nationalism, in which he had united the nation culturally while leading the movements to free the country from the slavery of the British.

Cultural unity is a civilizational vision of the national identity of our country. This is what cultural nationalism really is. The seeds of unity sprout amid this very diversity. Recognizing the strength of the country's diversity, Mahatma Gandhi worked to unite the nation for the freedom movement with the idea of equality. Keeping the nation paramount, he ensured the participation of the common people in his agitations. For him independence was not limited to freedom from British slavery, rather his emphasis was on the establishment of Swaraj throughout the country. Therefore, on the pretext of adopting Swadeshi, he also suggested the way to love the nation and the things and culture associated with it.

This aspect of Gandhiji has always impressed me that instead of opposing the other side, he associated politics with creation and tolerance. Activities like spinning yarn on the spinning wheel, boycotting foreign goods were not about the opposition to the other side, rather they were directly concerned with creation and Satyagraha was about tolerance. During the freedom movement, by awakening mutual harmony among the people of the country, he initiated a positive change in the public mind. In a way, he was developing a democratic culture in the country even during the times of slavery.

His origin of just politics appears to be related to cultural nationalism. The reason being, according to the Indian culture, emphasis was laid on, not getting angry with the opposition because of their immoral acts but developing the ability to tolerate them. The British knew the strategies as to how to keep the country in slavery for a long time. That is why, they would make people fight each other in the name of sect, casteism, and religion and often incited people for immoral violence by instigating them. Under its guise, they used to suppress those who fought in the freedom movement. It was their moral pattern of suppressing the rebellion by the British Raj. This is what the British had been doing to slave India for years. That is why freedom deluded India many times. But Gandhiji made a political entry into the freedom movement through the Champaran Satyagraha in such a way that under his leadership, people neither resorted to violence nor rebelled against the state. In 1917, when Gandhiji was banned by the British government during the Indigo Movement, the point of view that he presented before the judge still lingers in my mind. He said, "I have broken the law. You can punish me for this, But I have the right to move throughout my country." This fearless, non-violent way of presenting his rational point of view became the major mantra for the freedom movement later. Due to his rational arguments and the non-violent method of protest, the British eventually had to bow down to the Champaran movement. The Champaran movement gave the country that path through Gandhiji, in which the violent and non-violent aspects of the isolated country were completely organized in the form of a freedom movement. This made non-violence an effective weapon against the British Raj.

State violence is considered lawful and public violence is considered rebellion. It is not difficult to quell rebellion considering it immoral. Because in many ways immorality also enters the rebellion often. In such a situation, the state gets the weapon of morality to suppress the violence of the people. This is what the British always did under the guise of their rule. Gandhiji knew this, Therefore, he provided the moral courage to the people of the country to counter the violence of the state with non-violence which has been the tradition of Indian culture. His weapon of non-violence was such that all the justifications of state oppression were defeated. Even after this, if the people are oppressed, then the state's morality is at stake. In this way, Gandhiji worked to mentally incapacitate the British. This was the origin of Satyagraha, the civil non-cooperation movement, and non-violent protests. Therefore, the country's fight against the British under his leadership was decisive and the country could get independence.

A major aspect of Gandhi's freedom movement was that he brought social reform to the centre for political independence. He developed a sense of communality. That's why I also think that he had a vision of cultural nationalism that went beyond religion, caste, community, language, gender discrimination. It was thinking which contained the values of permanent freedom in a hate-free society. This is his broad vision of just politics. He has repeatedly said that a political movement cannot succeed without social reforms. That is why Gandhiji cannot be said to be associated with any particular party. In the prevailing circumstances of those times, he accepted the views he thought were in the interest of the country. He also expressed his dissatisfaction unhesitatingly at the views he did not find in the interest of the country. Gandhi's goal was not limited to the liberation of the country from the slavery of the British but also to make. the country completely independent in such a way that the interest of the person standing in the last line could also be made a part of the policy-making. He wanted to make the nation as inclusive as it could be. In view of the unity in diversity of the country, it is only in Gandhi's non-violent path of *Antyodaya*, equality, and taking everyone along, that his thinking in cultural nationalism and equitable politics can be deeply understood.

❑

16.

Subhash Chandra Bose
The Great Hero of the Freedom Movement

Subhash Chandra Bose formed the Azad Hind Army and gave the slogan - 'You give me blood; I will give you freedom'. Through that, he not only gave the youth the mantra to dedicate their lives to the nation but also did great work for the unity of the whole country. As a hero of the freedom movement, he carried out the important task of unifying the whole country under the flag of 'The Azad Hind Army'. I think he needs to be remembered as a hero of the freedom struggle, who crushed the 'Divide and Rule' policy of the British and erased the differences of provincialism along with those of religions and castes, and instilled the spirit of nationalism in the country.

Subhas Chandra Bose was a great man. His personality has always fascinated me. He was a man of his words and never made any distinction between words and deeds. He left his job under the British because of his immense love for the country. Later, he joined politics with the inspiration of Bengal's patriot Chittaranjan Das. He also went to jail for participating in the non-cooperation movement with Gandhiji. However, he had opposed the Gandhi-Irwin Pact but at its core was his vision of making the nation strong in the then circumstances. He wanted to realise his dream of making the country a socialist republic with absolute freedom for complete and all-around development. He emphasized organizing the peasants and labourers, boycotting the caste system by organizing the youth into volunteer groups under strict discipline, and especially giving top priority to the participation of women. He did that too at his level. With regard to the Gandhi-Irwin Pact, he said that one cannot doubt the patriotism of those who are responsible for the terms of this treaty; however, along with the unity and prosperity of the nation, there should be a strong demand for independence.

There was a reason why he was called *'Netaji'* (leader). At the core of this was his leadership quality of taking everyone along, in which people would not see any difference in the words and deeds of the leader. He always did what he said. He gave a powerful slogan like 'You give me blood; I will give you freedom' only to instill fervour among the youth for the independence of the country. That led to a wave of patriotism in the whole country.

Subhas Chandra Bose was such a great hero of freedom,

who, awakened the fervour among the youth, worked at his level to free the country not only from slavery of the British but also at all levels. He gave a message to the youth, 'Take a comprehensive look at life during the formative years of your life. Prepare for the struggle that lies ahead for you in the future.' He led the youth movement at five levels. They were - to empower youth politically, awaken social and economic responsibility in them, and always keep them physically and culturally alert.

In order to ensure the participation of women in the freedom movement along with their education and development, he also created a separate battalion 'The Rani of Jhansi Regiment'. He said, "When a woman is educated, the family and society will be educated and evil practices and superstitions in the country will end. Awareness in the country and society can be maintained only when women advance in every field. The aim of the women's regiment in the Azad Hind Army is to make women independent and strong."

I feel that it was Subhash Chandra Bose who gave a new identity to the development of women in the country. I have read his letters to his friends and family members during his stay in Rangoon, Mandalay, and Insein Jails. In them, his broad vision of working for the country and the society as well as staying pure both from inside and outside is revealed. He also had a close relationship with Rajasthan. I also learned that Subhash was an inspiration for Arjunlal Sethi and other freedom fighters of Rajasthan. During the princely period, when the artillery was deployed around Sikar, Subhash Chandra Bose intervened and gave full support to the people of Sikar. For this reason, in Sikar, people started addressing the area in front of the fortress as Subhash Chowk and it is known by this name even today.

Subhas Chandra Bose was in favour of complete independence. The slogan of his target was- 'Jai Hind', which means India should win in all areas. The dream of establishing India again as a world teacher was implicit in his thinking related to Indian culture and teachings. He also said that India is the foundation stone of the world's building. The world can stand on this foundation only. There is a need to work separately on his thinking of liberating the country along with its all-round development and making the country a superpower across the world. He was a great man and a great hero inside out.

❑

17.

Gautam Buddha

Lord Buddha, the Originator of the Wheel of Dharma

Buddha literally means - One who has attained perfect knowledge and who has become free from the cycle of birth and death. Lord Buddha was not a great soul or a saint only because of that, rather he was incarnated in the form of God and showed a path to remove the miseries of this world. He underwent severe penance. That was how he attained enlightenment. Enlightenment means inner awakening. It means that light which illuminates not only you but also others. The Buddha, being completely free from desires, cravings, and attachments, therefore gave the message to people to gain victory over themselves rather than seeking victory in battles. He gave us the means to conquer hatred with love. He called for sharing happiness to be happy and gave a life message of high ideals to focus only on the present instead of delving into the past and improving the future. I think that this message of Lord Buddha is equally relevant today as much as it was during his time.

Buddha was also called *'Mahabhishak'*, which means doctor - the person who can remove our suffering. Lord Shiva is also called *'Mahabhishak'* or *Vaidyanath*. Shiva means one who drinks poison for others, who takes away all the sufferings of others. This is what Buddha did in his life. He left the royal palace in search of knowledge. We see immense compassion in the idols where he is in meditating pose.

Maharishi Aurobindo had also said that the compassion seen in Buddha's idols is the goal of Buddha's *sadhana* (meditation), in which there is a sense of universal welfare and not personal *nirvana* (emancipation). That expression on his face appeared with the desire to remove the suffering of others after seeing it.

Lord Buddha seems even more relevant during this frightful period of Covid. His message about finding our happiness in the happiness of others with his service, dedication, and sacrifice is needed more in this time. We celebrate Buddha Purnima or Buddha Jayanti on the full moon day of Vaishakh month. Buddha Purnima is also very important because on this day special energy is infused into the atmosphere. It is said that the moon greatly affects the earth and the water element on a full moon night. According to astrology, the moon is considered to be the lord of *Purnima Tithi*; so, Buddha Purnima is also considered the day to get freedom from all kinds of mental problems. Lord Buddha attained enlightenment under the *Peepal* tree. That is why worshiping the *Peepal* tree on this day has great significance.

I believe that Buddha Purnima is not just the birth anniversary of Lord Buddha. It has deep implications. Buddha Purnima means – a holy day to bow down to the light of knowledge. This day is also sacred and important because it is on this day that Buddha was born, attained enlightenment, and left this world.

In some of our Puranas, Lord Vishnu has been described as an incarnation of Buddha. When the distance between human beings started growing and when human and animal sacrifices in the name of Vedic Yagya were at their peak, exploitation of common people increased in the name of rituals, Lord Vishnu himself, the protector of the Vedas, appeared in the incarnated form of Buddha and illuminated the ideal of life. What would be a better example of the sublimity of *Sanatan Dharma* than this!

Buddha wanted everyone's sorrow to be removed from the world and that no one should suffer. That is why he also said that instead of feeling sad upon seeing someone unhappy, we should work towards enabling and empowering them. This is the Bodhisattva. While preaching the Gita, Lord Krishna had told Arjuna, *'Bahunam Janamnamante Gyanvan Maam Prapadyate'*, which means, it is only a result of the practice of knowledge for many births that a man becomes knowledgeable and attains God. This is what happened in the case of Buddha. He attained enlightenment i.e., 'Buddhahood' under the Bodhi tree. The enlightenment that the Buddha attained was only after the continuous spiritual practice of many Bodhisattvas and many Bodhisattva lives. That is why Buddha came to be known as Lord Buddha in our country.

The life of Buddha is also a unique example of ideals. The divine child Siddhartha who was born from the womb of Mayadevi, the wife of King Suddhodana of Kapilavastu was raised by stepmother Gautami. Since Gautami had brought him up, he was also called Gautama. After he attained Buddhahood, the prefix Buddha was added to his name. He was called Lord Buddha because he attained God by being enlightened. Buddha taught us the middle path of life. The middle way means avoiding all kinds of excesses. He meditated under the tree for seven days and seven nights. His resolve was that he would remain in the meditative position till he attained knowledge. He attained enlightenment on the eighth day on *Vaishakh Purnima* and became *Tathagata* on the same day. The tree under which he attained enlightenment is still known as the 'Bodhi tree'. The Bodhi tree is a revered Peepal tree.

The first sermon that the Buddha delivered at Sarnath is called *Dhammachakra Pravartan* (the turning of the wheel of Dharma). As per Buddhist beliefs, this is the '*Dhammachak*'. It literally means 'the wheel of religion'. Buddha taught the Eightfold Path as a means of getting rid of suffering and knowing facts. All its paths begin with the word *'Samyak'*. *Samyak* means right. In Buddhist symbolism, the eight paths are often represented by the eight rods of the *Dharmachakra*. This Dharmachakra is also one of the *Ashtmangals* recognized in Indian culture. In the Puranas, only 24 sages could receive the full power of Gayatri. The 24 characters of Gayatri Mantra represent these 24 sages. Chakra is also mentioned in the verses of the Bhagavad Gita. Buddha also spoke about 24 qualities to his disciples. In the middle of the national flag of our country, the Dharmachakra is in the form of the Ashoka Chakra, which is represented by 24 spokes. This chakra is a symbol of progress and life.

Just as we consider Lord Krishna as the 'Founder of Dharma', Rama is recognized in the Sanatan tradition as *'Ramo Vigrahavan Dharmah'* (Lord Rama is Dharma incarnate). In the same way, Lord Buddha is known as *'Dharmachakra Pravartak'* (Turner of the Wheel of Dharma).

Buddha is God because he is eternal. His teachings are also the message for an ideal life. He contemplated about only one thing and that was that everyone's sorrow in the world should be eradicated forever. He also constantly said in his messages that instead of becoming sad upon seeing someone's suffering, it is better to make that person capable and empowered. In the Sanatan tradition, the meaning of God is the one who removes our sorrows and sufferings. Therefore, it would not be an exaggeration to call Shiva, Rama, Krishna, Buddha, and Mahavira as *Panchparameshwar* (five gods).

❑

18.

Maharana Pratap
Vociferous nationalist Maharana Pratap

I consider Maharana Pratap as the first freedom fighter warrior of our country. He was a hero of the freedom struggle, who for the sake of the freedom of his motherland gave up the splendour of the royal palace and chose to live in the valleys of Aravalli and inaccessible forests. He never bowed his head regarding the terms of the independence of the nation.

Maharana Pratap's struggle for independence was not ordinary. It was a struggle, in which, Rana while living with the tribal and forest-dwelling Bhils and leading life like them, not only fought wars with the Mughals on every front but also defeated them repeatedly. For full 25 years, he fought with Akbar's army which was in large numbers with his brave soldiers who were very few in numbers. But his rare organizational power, guerrilla tactics like that of

Shivaji's, and his technique of making the enemy give up by discouraging it instead of using force, always kept him at the forefront of the war.

During the freedom struggle, Lala Lajpat Rai had once said that if the youth were to be prepared for the independence of India, then they would have to take inspiration from a history maker like *Veer Shiromani* Maharana Pratap. In the light of his statement, it would not be an exaggeration to say that Maharana Pratap was a great example of powerful nationalism. I also believe that his struggle for the independence of his motherland Mewar was based on that constitutionalism of imperialism and independence, in which national love, self-respect could be deeply felt. If he had wanted, he could have lived a life of luxury. Akbar himself was dazed by his bravery. He wanted to let him remain the king of Mewar under him, but the Rana did not accept it. History is witness that he had sent out a clear message to Akbar as to why he should get the right of the land which did not belong to him. Therefore, in the name of Mewar, he raised the flag of self-respect for the nation by awakening enthusiasm among the people for the independence of the nation.

The great thing about Maharana Pratap's freedom struggle was his moral and character strength. Among his subjects and military force, he gave more importance to the moral values of freedom. There was no difference between his words and deeds. That's why he sent this message, especially among the common people that this fight is not his alone, but of all the people who love the motherland. Therefore, he publicly took a pledge to renounce the royal glories and not to eat food in vessels of gold and silver until Mewar became completely independent. Accordingly, the people were informed about this through public announcements. Due to this, it was natural that the subjects joined him in the struggle for freedom wholeheartedly. To fight Akbar's large army, he organized the Bhils and tribals along with the common people on his own. Calling for the struggle not against Akbar but for the independence of the motherland, he himself went and asked for cooperation by befriending the Bhils. And he did receive a lot of support. The forest dwellers supported Maharana Pratap in the form of spies, soldiers, and guards in the mountains and secret caves. Keeping aside mutual animosity, he built friendly relations with Rajput kings and fellow chieftains and made them aware of the impending crisis. His close relations with the Chauhans of Bundi, Dungarpur, Banswara, Ranthambore, the Deoras of Idar and Sirohi, and a few other kings can be seen in this perspective.

I feel that if any national hero has given inspiration to our country to sacrifice our life while being committed to the nation and fighting for it, then it is none other than Maharana Pratap. His sublime character always inspired fellow warlords. Everyone knows, Mansingh had become the chief warlord of Akbar. It was natural that he was the biggest enemy of the Rana. Once when he went hunting with only a few soldiers, he was caught by Maharana Pratap. If he had wanted, he could have attacked Mansingh and killed him at that time, but he did not do so displaying his bigheartedness. Through this, he also gave a message to the Rajput kings that everyone should give up mutual animosity and fight unitedly for the motherland.

Maharana Pratap had a very strong character. He had an innate respect for women. I have experienced this over and over again by reading about him in history. Once Kunwar Amar Singh defeated the enemy at Sherpur and brought women from Abdul Rahim Khan-e-Khana's camp along with the soldiers who were taken prisoner in the war. When Maharana Pratap came to know about it, he was very angry. He ordered the immediate release of the captured women and children and directed them to be sent respectfully to the camp of Abdul Rahim Khan-e-Khana. Abdul Rahim Khan-i-Khana was so impressed by this benevolent behaviour of Rana that he gave up his enmity and animosity against Mewar forever. In this manner, Maharana won everyone over with his lofty values.

In fact, Akbar with his imperialistic ambitions wanted to rule the whole of Mewar. His influence was so great that all the kings of the princely states around Mewar had taken refuge under Akbar. Maharana Pratap's brother Jagmal had taken refuge under the Mughal Subedar of Ajmer. Later another brother Shakti Singh also joined Akbar's court. Maharana Pratap was also repeatedly given a message that he did not have to do anything and that he would remain the ruler; he should just accept Mughal subjugation. But

Rana never accepted it. His fight was not with the Mughals, rather it was with the ideology of imperialism, under which Akbar wanted to subjugate the entire nation. That's why Maharana Pratap, with his valour and courage, stirred up strong nationalism throughout the country. Even today, his fight for love for the motherland is a unique example of ideal in Indian history.

❑

19.

Baba Saheb Ambedkar
Sublime Vision of Social Democracy

Whenever I think about Babasaheb Ambedkar's thoughts and his sublime vision, his work for social democracy starts flashing in my mind. It was not a mere coincidence that when the last meeting of the Constituent Assembly took place, Babasaheb Ambedkar's address had social democracy at its centre. He said that the caste system and democracy cannot co-exist. Therefore, certain guidelines were introduced in the Indian Constitution, which stated that there should be no discrimination on the basis of caste and language for the citizens living in any part of the country.

I believe that any nation is formed by its traditions, culture, religion, castes, and languages. Hence there is no place for narrow-mindedness in nationalism. The main responsibility of proving the provisions of the draft and giving justification for them in the Constituent Assembly lay with Dr. Ambedkar and other 'Draft Committee' members. In a way, he gave voice to the country's traditions, faith, and belief in the constitution which he had drafted with the help of his skilled colleagues. But the basic point in it was that all the citizens of the country are Indians first and their other identities came later.

If we delve deeper into the statements given by Dr. Ambedkar in the Constituent Assembly, we will also find that there is a unique amalgamation of politics, law, history, philosophy in them. There is a sense of equality for all and not just for anyone caste. In November 1948, while presenting his proposal to consider the draft of the constitution, he said that we have called India not a union of states, but a union state. I believe that Dr. Ambedkar was concerned about the social division in India. That is why he had said that if we want to build democracy, then we have to recognize the obstacles in our path. A grand palace of the Constitution can stand in a democracy only if it is built on the foundation of loyalty of the people.

I think Dr. Ambedkar's thoughts are actually linked to that nationalism, in which there is no distinction between individuals with regard to caste, class, and religion. Every citizen of the country is equal in principle. There is harmony among all of us under the social system and social thinking. That is why our nation is an excellent example of unity in diversity. That is why equality and fraternity for all citizens have been talked about in the Preamble of the Indian Constitution.

From this point of view, Dr. Ambedkar has also explained Indianism from a broader perspective in his thoughts. While giving importance to the land, its society, and its finest traditions for nation-building, he also emphasized that the nation is not a physical unit. The nation is the result of continuous efforts, sacrifice, and patriotism of the people of the past. Describing the nation as a living entity, he also said that nationalism is social consciousness and due to this people come closer to each other. That is how the feeling of fraternity develops. The thoughts of narrow-mindedness are the biggest obstacle in this. He clearly said that I want all the people of India to consider themselves as only Indians. If for some reason this does not happen, then we will be committing the biggest sin and I will always oppose it with all my might.

As the architect of the Indian Constitution, Dr. Ambedkar borrowed three words from the French Revolution – Liberty, Equality, and Fraternity. These words included in the core of the constitution also deeply influenced his political and social life philosophy. Therefore, in the Fundamental Rights of the Constitution, there is an explanation of the right to equality through Articles 14 to 18.

In this regard, the right to freedom has been given through Articles 19 to 22 of the Constitution and the right against exploitation has been given in Articles 23 and 24. It is also an important fact that the right to freedom of expression in Article 19(2) has been restricted to any unrestrained expression against any caste, class, or community. Under the Constitution, it should not in any way harm the security, sovereignty, and integrity of the country. If there is a law or is being constituted for the protection of these three things, then it should not be hindered. The right to freedom of religion has been given in the Indian Constitution through Articles 25 to 28. I believe that the Constitution of India is one of the constitutions around the world, in which the fundamental rights have been explained in this way.

Dr. Ambedkar's thoughts had a deep influence as he advanced with an original vision in almost all fields. If we delve into his thoughts related to women's education, it will seem that, to some extent, he was the initial facilitator to initiate a reservation for women in jobs. While addressing a women's meeting in Bombay, he had once said that women are the builders of the nation, that every citizen grows up in her lap and that without awakening women, the development of the nation is not possible. If we delve deeper into his thoughts, we will also find that he was probably the first scholar in India who tried to understand the position of women within the caste framework from the point of view of gender. For this, he systematically advocated for women's rights. His basic vision was how equality could be established at all levels of society. That's why he laid constant emphasis on making society classless. His thought that always illuminates the mind was 'revolution is for the people, people are not for the revolution'.

Dr. Ambedkar was a great personality. Therefore, binding him with narrow-mindedness is an attempt to weaken his personality. I also believe that it is a reflection of intellectual poverty to associate him with any particular class or caste. He was a great man with a sublime vision. The lofty ideal of seeing everyone as equal in his thoughts revolved around the all-around development of the nation. The role he played in nation-building also needs to be explained in a broader sense. It also needs to be understood that Article D-370 was also added against his wish in the Constitution, which has been removed after 72 years of independence through the strong will and determination of the present Prime Minister Shri Narendra Modi and Home Minister Shri Amit Shah. Instead of looking at his holistic thinking and vision in a lopsided manner, there is a need to consider them holistically and deeply.

If we delve deeply into Dr. Ambedkar's thoughts, it will also appear that they contain seeds of equality along with the unity and integrity of the country. Therefore, his philosophy of *'Bahujan Hitay, Bahujan Sukhay'* (for the happiness of the many, for the welfare of the many) along with equality and justice is relevant even today and it will remain relevant in the future as well.

❑

20.

Pandit Deendayal Upadhyay
The Architect of 'Integral Humanism'

Pandit Deendayal Upadhyay was a personality with multifaceted talent. He had the qualities of an educationist, politician, fierce speaker, writer, and journalist. He gave a new *ism* to India in addition to the many *isms* prevalent in the world. His all-encompassing *ism* was the principle of 'Integral Humanism'. It is a practical and philosophical principle. In a way, this was the mantra given by Pandit Deendayal Upadhyay to see the human being in its entirety.

Deendayal Upadhyay was a *pracharak* of the Rashtriya Swayamsevak Sangh from the very beginning. When the Bharatiya Jana Sangh was formed in the year 1950, he started working in the Jana Sangh. At that time, Dr. Shyamprasad Mookerjee had said, "If I can get a couple of more workers like Deendayal Upadhyaya, I can change the politics of the country."

I agree that Upadhyay Ji was an expert in the art of connecting people. Perhaps that was the reason why when Dr. Mookerjee died under suspicious circumstances in Sri Nagar within 2 years of the establishment of Jana Sangh, and many people felt that Jana Sangh would not survive without him, Deendayal Ji proved this apprehension unfounded and Jana Sangh started moving on the path of progress. Deendayal Upadhyay together with Ram Manohar Lohia wanted to create a platform for the nationalist forces in the country. Deendayalji had prepared the ground for the nationalist forces, as a result of which, the nationalist forces were established on the axis of the country's politics by the end of the twentieth century.

There was another reason behind the fame of Deendayalji. When he introduced the concept of Integral Humanism, there was a lot of discussion on it. It became the subject of heated debate in universities and intellectual institutions. To agree or not to agree was a different matter, but it was difficult for the intellectual world to disregard integral humanism. Deendayal Upadhyay established the concept of Integral Humanism by reflecting on the fundamental questions about human behaviour, individual and society, and human development. In fact, since ancient times, thinkers all over the world have been contemplating human being. All thinkers claim to be devoted to the development and happiness of human beings. But before thinking in this direction, it is also necessary to understand the human mind. If the human mind is properly understood, then only the paths for happiness and development can be determined. This has been happening in the West as well as in India.

The West claimed to have understood the human mind. Those thinkers concluded that man is a social animal. He cannot live alone; his happiness and sorrow are connected with the happiness and sorrow of thesociety. Other thinkers rejected it. They concluded that man is an economic creature. He is social only till it serves his financial interests. The attainment of the basic necessities for survival is the goal of a man and he gets happiness from that. Some thinkers of the West rejected this as well. According to him, human behaviour is actually driven by work. Everything else is secondary. These conclusions of western thinkers make sense if brought together, they do not really stand a chance when considered unilaterally. . But western thinkers are not ready to accept this. That's why all the theories of anthropology that they coined were coined by considering only one factor as the main one. The concepts of capitalism and communism were actually formed based on material factors. The kind of damage that could have been brought about by these concepts and principles is being suffered by the West.

The concept of Integral Humanism established by Deendayal Upadhyay is based on India's ancient cultural thought. Upadhyayji believed that socialism, capitalism, or communism, in other words, economism or materialism basically creates more deviation and gives fewer solutions. Human beings are not meant to fit into the fixed framework of capitalism or communism. The basic concept should be of humanism and all other theories or principles should be created keeping humans at the centre. But the opposite is happening in the West. The proponents of economism have created theories and are now forcing human beings to mould themselves based on these imaginary principles.

Humanism or the development of human beings cannot be seen in fragments, it requires an integral vision. Human beings need all kinds of things. He needs society as well as fulfillment of basic needs and also music-literature-art in the field of work. But keep in mind that he needs it all together. Perhaps that is why Deendayal Upadhyayji has called the path of human development or humanism integral. Integral Humanism talks about the holistic development of the human being. Deendayal Upadhyay is used to explain this with the help of the ancient Indian concept of *Purushartha Chatushtya*. Indian thinkers have discussed four *Purusharthas* (object of human pursuit) – Dharma (righteousness, moral values), *Artha* (prosperity, economic values), *Kama* (pleasure, love, psychological values), and *Moksha* (liberation, spiritual values). But these four *Purusharthas* are not separate, they are intertwined. Man will make the efforts to achieve *Artha* (prosperity, economic values), *Kama* (pleasure, love, psychological values), but religion has drawn a line for performing actions in both these areas. One more thing has to be kept in mind that while making efforts to achieve all kinds of *Purusharthas* (object of human pursuit), there should be some goal for human life. Indian thinkers have called this goal '*Moksha*' (liberation, spiritual values).

To explain the concept of integral, Deendayalji used to give another example of a relationship. One person maintains many relationships at the same time. He is a father, brother, son at the same time. All these relations are connected to each other. This is the harmony of human nature. Man is a child, then youth, and finally, he becomes old. But these three states of man form a complete unit. The West may have overlooked this wholeness of human beings and looked at it from a fragmented perspective and created models of development. Deendayal Upadhyay introduced the Indian model of human development as an alternative to these models, which is known in the intellectual society as Integral Humanism. Through the concept of Integral Humanism, Deendayal Upadhyay has touched the Achilles heel of today's one-sided development models. The ultimate aim of all of the activities that man carries out and whatever kind of development models he implements is to get happiness or satisfaction.

The believers in economism think that happiness comes from more enjoyment, but Deendayalji gave an example and said that happiness depends on the state of mind. That is why he advocated the holistic concept of development, in which there was a coordination between the development of the mind, intellect, and body.

Today, when the principles of indulgent development are leading to the deterioration of happiness all over the world and the very existence of human beings is threatened due to improper usage of resources, the relevance of the Integral Humanism of Deendayal Upadhyay has increased even more.

The great thinker and great man Pandit Deendayal Upadhyayji dedicated his life to the service of the people. We can pay true tribute to Panditji only by imbibing his ideals and participating actively in social service. Panditji's Indian value-based simple lifestyle is an inspiration for all of us.

He had profound social thoughts on national interest and nurturing people. Panditji believed that human beings have a social, economic, and political life. According to the Indian view, man is the combination of body, mind, intellect, and soul. All four have their own needs, for the fulfillment of which a person has to make efforts. A system of easy availability from society has to be ensured. That is Integral Humanism. Everyone should get food, every hand should get work and every field should get water. It is such priorities that move society forward and then happiness and peace are established among the people. Pandit Deendayal was a progressive thinker. He remained grounded.

❑

21.

National Security and Pandit Deendayal Upadhyay

For any nation and state, the matter of national security is of paramount importance among all the issues of national interests. For the common man, national security is synonymous with the national interest, which means he considers that by protecting the geographical boundaries of the country, unity and integrity are kept safe. The traditional definition of national security confined it to the military and strategic dimensions. The reason for reinforcing this view has been that no state which is unable to maintain unity, integrity, and geographical boundaries free from aggressive violations can consider itself sovereign. If it cannot consolidate its authority on the territory shown on the map within its jurisdiction, which is recognized as a nation-state, then it is considered to be subordinate.

It is often overlooked why this military and strategic security is considered so important. The fact is that in domestic politics within the boundaries of the nation-state, autonomy is required to implement economic policies, choose a political system, and maintain order in social organization as it desires, and for that sovereign hegemony in any particular territory is necessary. Attempts to protect their economic, social and cultural national interests through military-strategic security are considered national interests. It is worth repeating that the economic and social aspects of national security cannot be considered less important than the military aspects.

Some scholars believe that it is inherent in the word 'Strategic/Military'. A scholar named Walter, through a very succinct comment has clarified that a nation can be considered secure only as long as it cannot be compelled to sacrifice its basic values. These values, which are associated with its existence and are part of its national identity, should, when challenged, require no compromise in the event of war being rejected, and in the event of war being fought (for their protection), its victory should be ensured. This intangible aspect of national security is the least understood and perhaps the most important.

Today, when many forces are working to destabilize and disintegrate the country, if we do not deliberate on how to deal with this problem, we may have to face serious consequences. We also have to warn the world about this problem so that there can be an established classification of 'Break India' forces operating in India and abroad.

Civilization and culture give us a common identity, a shared historical heritage, and a future. It makes us aware that our country and this culture deserve to be fought for and protected. Breaking a civilization is like breaking the backbone of a person. A broken civilization can shatter to pieces and throw an entire region into deep darkness.

Does Indian civilization tend to break down like this? And what are those forces, which are trying to break it? Are they external forces or internal? Or both? Where do they originate, how do they grow? Who operates them? What are the central forces holding India together? Much is being written and said about economic development, commercial and industrial development, and better democratic governance. But there is little discussion about the internal and external decentralized forces that have the power to break India.

But the external forces breaking the country are more complex and they are creating an equation with our internal rifts. There is a worldwide system, which is controlling these internal forces. Pakistan is not the only one spreading disorder in our country nor are China's relations with Maoists or converting forces of Europe and America the only elements spreading separatism. These elements are definitely problematic. However, more worrisome than these is that all these divisive forces have a deep and complex interrelationship.

The path of Pandit Deendayal Upadhyay

In the interrelationship, the path of Pandit Deendayal Upadhyay is the lit path of humanity. If we delve deeper into his philosophy, it will also appear that he was a strong advocate of lofty values of life under 'Integral Humanism'. If we take a brief look at his thoughts, we will also get answers to the questions related to the security of the nation.

Rashtra Devo Bhavah (Nation is equivalent to God)

Deendayalji said that there can be no compromise as far as the unity and integrity of the country are concerned. The unity and integrity of the country is a matter of our faith and we will strive to achieve that. He said, *'Rashtra Devo Bhavah'* - our nation is like our god. When all the citizens of the nation start accepting this, then most of the problems of the country will be solved. No obstacle will come in the way of resolving national challenges. If a little trouble appears somewhere on the way, everybody will complement each other because everyone will advance with the idea of one nation.

Defense is a continual inevitability

At the time of China's invasion, the task of explaining the importance of self-defence to the country fell on Deendayalji. He had to issue repeated warnings about this crisis until the invasion by China in 1962. When Deendayalji supported the Dalai Lama, all the so-called progressive people ridiculed

Deendayalji asking if he is really a Dalai Lama. They called him weak-spirited Lama. Deendayalji ignored the scorn. In a country where Veer Savarkar who had fought hard for the country's defense was called a recruit hero, it was no surprise that the Jana Sangh was called battle-hungry. But Deendayalji, who thought only of the national interest, continued the demand for defense-readiness without falling into the trap of cheap popularity or misleading slogans.

After the Chinese invasion, Deendayalji put forth Jana Sangh's demand that an atomic bomb is made and declared that any price to be paid for the defense of freedom is small. For 10 years from 1952 to 1962, Deendayalji continuously warned about China and held many demonstrations. When China launched a big attack, the people of the country understood the importance of his work very well. America helped us during the Chinese invasion of 1962, but Russia remained aloof. The blood relations are closer, but only three months after that, Deendayalji made a prediction. If we carefully analyze the expansionist policies of China, then not only some nations of Asia but also some communist countries will criticize the expansionism of China and join us.

What will be the cost of defense? This is the answer to this question as well. A nation should spend on defense as much as is necessary. Where to get the money from? It should be saved in the same way as it was saved for security material to date. There is no alternative for defense. The alternatives like dialogues, *Panchsheel*, peace discourse, etc. have proved fatal. Therefore, today the real need is to stockpile weapons, compulsory military education, politics that teaches people to be ready for possible war and toil hard to maintain the independence of the motherland even if the basic needs have to be put aside. These four formulae are necessary today.

Defence-readiness

China carried out a nuclear explosion and entered the club of nuclear weapon-owning countries. Pandit Deendayalji Upadhyay organized a massive demonstration by mobilizing a mass movement by Jana Sangh. There was a tide of self-defence and patriotism in the country. Lakhs of protesters from every corner reached Delhi. Just a month later, war broke out with Pakistan. For the first time in history, the Indian Army made the general public realize that these lines from a poem 'Without war, who has got freedom? Where is freedom without war?' is absolutely true.

Foreign policy and home sdefense both are complementary

Pandit Deendayal Upadhyay said that both the foreign policy and the self-defence of the country are related. Now, this policy should be determined only based on conclusions of protecting and nurturing national interests. Pandit Deendayal Upadhyaya's thoughts about foreign policy and self-defence were totally based on national interest. Along with political leaders like Veer Savarkar, Subhash Chandra Bose, and Dr. Munje, his thoughts also provided guidance.

Deendayalji used these ideas as weapons in his work related to foreign politics and defence. He found the phrase *'Shastren rakshite rashtre, shastra charcha pravartate'* to be completely exemplary. India has been naturally opposed to monopolism. Therefore, India should be in favour of the development of democracy and freedom in the world. Natural compassion should be shown towards the countries which are free from colonialism. Deendayalji said that India must make efforts for peace, but for the sake of peace, one should not do something that would disregard the country and cause it to suffer.

India should make nuclear weapons

In order to protect ourselves from the joint threat imposed by China and Pakistan, we must make nuclear weapons. Some have also commented on how making nuclear weapons will be an expensive burden on a poor country like ours. However, we have proved them wrong and are on our way to strengthening our defense system.

Emphasizing recruitment in the army, Shri Upadhyay said that the strength of the army should be increased to 20 lakhs. More people in the age group of twenty years should be recruited and the internal security forces should also be strengthened. The police force in the border areas should be under the central government and a separate border security police should be formed for that. All those elements whose loyalty to the country is doubtful should be kept at least 1 mile away from the border.

Jana Sangh's outlook toward China and Pakistan

The opinion of Bharatiya Jana Sangh is completely clear in this matter. It says that the invasions from both China and Pakistan should end. It has given utmost importance to border security. Jana Sangh literally supports the freedom of every inch of India's land. Its manifesto states that the borders of India have been encroached upon. Pakistan on one hand and China on the other have occupied a large area of our country. Despite the nation's ability to successfully repulse the attack, the Congress government has lowered the morale of the country as a result of its tax policy and has provided an opportunity to the enemy to strengthen its position. Bharatiya Jana Sangh will take up this challenge to the country's independence and sovereignty and will free every inch of India's territory.

It has reiterated its promise regarding Kashmir in the following words-

The Bharatiya Jana Sangh considers the attack on Kashmir as an attack on India and will therefore resort to every measure to liberate the territories occupied by Pakistan and China.

The Communists should not make a seditious attempt to divide the army

On the criticism of the loyalty of the army by the communists, Deendayalji said that to challenge the loyalty of the security services or to spread illusions about them is catastrophic for the nation (Degeneracy- degeneration of physical, mental, and moral qualities). Our forces have conducted themselves very well on every occasion. They have a laudable and proud history. It is a grave ingratitude to impose upon them the spirit of rebellion, even though it does not exist. If one thinks about them in this way, it only means that they have something suspicious in their minds.

Communists express the possibilities of a military revolution in the country, they thoughtlessly want to impose foreign moulds on the Indian situation. But it should be kept in mind that such steps have not been rejected in the communist system. If today the communists are discussing the possibility of a military revolution, then perhaps it is out of a sense of despair arising from the failure of their plans to hide their own intentions. If all these allegations are true, then the commander should be congratulated, not condemned. He has made a commendable effort to protect the apolitical stand of the army.

Learn to identify enemies and friends

Once, a circular issued by the All-India Congress Committee termed the opposition parties and especially the Bharatiya Jana Sangh and the Swatantra Party as anti-national for criticizing the government policies. The communists were lauded for being 100% nationalist, while the Jana Sangh and the Swatantra Party were declared anti-nationals. Deendayalji said that the Congress party has some unique standards. All we can say is that we have complete and undivided allegiance towards only Mother India; apart from this, we have no allegiance to anyone else. If we have committed any crime, then it is that we have been saying those things for many years what the Prime Minister and Congress leaders are saying today. He said that the friend gives a warning whereas the enemy attacks. With this utmost spirit of selfless devotion to the motherland, we should dedicate ourselves to the defence of freedom.

The issue of national security should be given paramount importance

External aggression or any other internal crisis can become a cause of disaster for the unity and integrity of any nation. Similarly, if a country is economically decrepit, then it soon becomes a victim of external aggression. But as a result of external aggression, a strong sentiment of nationalism has also arisen. That's why it is also called a boon in times of crisis. According to an English proverb, though such a nation survives in times of war the time of peace is like death for it.

However, based on this logic one cannot conceive or plan a war. However, every nation must be always ready for self-defence, both from a military and psychological perspective because, without this, no nation can maintain its independence in the world for a long time. Additionally, apart from preparing for self-defense against external aggression, a nation should also be prepared to face the disintegrations and separatist elements within the country. But if there is any political party in the country, which is indifferent to the unity and integrity of the nation, then it is neither possible for it to face the disruptive elements nor can it counter the enemy. In fact, such a party that is so indifferent toward security cannot be successful in maintaining the survival of the nation.

Unlike all these political parties, Jana Sangh was the only party at that time, which was suspicious of China. Pakistan had stated in its election manifesto of 1951 that the northern frontier of India also was not secure. Ignoring India's peaceful approach, China has enslaved Tibet by destroying its independence, which is against the policy of coexistence. Even while signing a treaty with Nepal, China did not take into account the special position of India. Similarly, India should be cautious regarding China's activities such as showing the Indian region on the maps of China and claiming that it was done by mistake, entry of Chinese armies there (it was claimed to have happened due to misunderstanding), and Chinese activities in small countries of South-East Asia. It is clear from this that Jana Sangh did not make any mistake at that time in understanding the Chinese. In 1957, except for the Jana Sangh, all other political parties were indifferent toward the security of the nation and were giving importance only to political and economic programmes. But at that time, the Jana Sangh had called the issue of security to be of paramount importance and while giving its suggestions for it, it had said that along with expanding the country's army and instilling national feeling in it, it should be equipped with the latest weapons.

Jana Sangh had also suggested compulsory military training for the youth. Knowing that the State Governments could not make proper security arrangements for the frontier areas, Jan Sangh had also suggested setting up a Frontier Police Establishment under the Centre. If the centre had already taken over the task of frontier inspection and security, the government would have come to know about the Chinese entry into Aksai Chin a long time ago.

Deendayal Ji used to say that we need warriors today, not just those who oppose. The integrity of the country cannot be protected by those who simply sit and make calculations. Only those who have faith and pride and who are determined to sacrifice everything for the sake of the motherland can fight with all their might.

❑

22.

Women are Pioneers Leading in Every Field

A woman is power personified. Calling her weak and helpless is to ignore that reality. This society, family, and life cannot be imagined without her. That is why I have always been interpreting women's empowerment not as a slogan, but as a social sense of accepting the existence of women.

Remember, the Oxford Dictionary selected 'woman power' as the most discussed word of the year two years ago. It was then accepted as the most used word around the world. The reason behind this was that the echo of the decisions taken keeping in view the development of women in India was heard all over the world. This brought women's empowerment to the centre of discussion and Oxford Dictionary declared 'Woman Power' as the most spoken about the term of the year. In the larger interest of women, big decisions related to triple talaq, allowing entry of women in Kerala's Sabarimala temple, allowing combat roles for women in the defence forces, allowing women wishing to go to Haj to go there without a male guardian could have been taken long ago in the country. But we were not willing to act on these issues while women have been playing the leading roles in society since the beginning. Isn't it our duty as well to think in their interest?

Women are far better than men at not only taking decisions sensitively but also at acting in the interest of the community. If their talent is given the opportunity, then they advance faster and pave the way for the development of the entire society. This is why Mahatma Gandhi once said that if one woman from a family gets educated, then two families benefit from it. Why was there a need for movements like *'Beti Bachao, Beti Padhao'* (Save girl child, educate girl child)? Because if the daughters are educated and remain a part of the society, then India can again walk on the path to becoming a superpower. I believe that it is the power of a woman that she works not only for herself but also keeps in view the welfare of the whole world. The real architect of the concept of *'Vasudhaiva Kutumbakam'* has been women's power.

If we refer to our ancient *Puranas* and *Shastras*, we will realise that this world is run only by the power of women. In the form of Saraswati, a woman is a creator. In the form of Lakshmi, she is is a nurturer. She destroys demonic powers in the form of Mahakali. There is also another aspect that Saraswati is the goddess of knowledge and education in the whole world. Imagine, if there is no knowledge, then how will this world continue to be illuminated? In the absence of knowledge and wisdom, man becomes animal-like. Similarly, Lakshmi is the goddess of wealth and prosperity. That is how all the functions in the world take place. In absence of *Shakti* (power) in the form of Durga, only evil forces will exist in the world. That is, this whole earth is surviving due to the goddess forms of women. Despite this, if we deny the existence of women's power, then there is no greater intellectual poverty.

In Indian culture, the tradition of *Kanya-Pujan* (girl worship) has been existing since the beginning. The nine days of *Chaitra Navratri* are meant for earning power for the whole year. All the powers reside in the nine Durgas; so, nine forms of the Mother Durga are worshiped and revered for nine days. It is through these nine forms that this world is moving. That is why I repeatedly say that without women's power, the development of humanity cannot be imagined. There is also a need that we rid society of the negative adjectives labeling women as weak and feeble. We should change our mindset that women need support. She is capable and self-reliant.

Instead of talking about the past, if we talk about the present, we will remember that Rakhi Paliwal of the Rajsamand district took the initiative to organize women against having to get up at four in the morning and go for defecation in the open. Positive results were seen shortly and women's power became the vehicle for a big campaign in society in the form of Rakhi. Fighter pilots Avani Chaturvedi, Bhawna, and Mohana Singh were selected for flying the supersonic fighter jet. Kalpana Chawla became the first woman to travel into space. Similarly, when women have got opportunities in every field, they have set an example in the country and society by trying to do their best.

In our country, we have worshiped *Shakti* (power) in the form of the Goddess, who is the symbol of victory and success. *Maryada Purushottam* Ram acquired power for victory by worshiping *Bhagwati Bhavani* before defeating Ravana. Shivaji acquired power by worshipping *Bhramamba Bhavani*. Maharana Pratap acquired power by worshipping *Chamunda* and launched the struggle for the freedom of the motherland. In every era, at all times, the woman's power has existed in the form of a goddess for the overall welfare of the nation. That is why she is a unique creation of God. She is as pure as the Ganges, as patient as the earth, and as firm as the Himalayas. If you read about successful women in modern contexts, then all these qualities will flash in front of your eyes.

Therefore, I believe that this is the time when there is a need to accept a woman's greatness and give an opportunity to her excellence in all fields rather than talking about women's equality. A man is successful only when there is a woman with him. He is able to achieve success because the woman who takes care of the family indirectly becomes the reason for his success in all the fields. Manusmriti says, *'Yatra narayastu pujyante ramante tatra devatah, yatrainastu na pujyante sarvastatraphalaha kriyah'* is self-evident because gods reside where women are worshiped. Where she is not respected, all the efforts are fruitless. She is the abode of god means that all the accomplishments and successes are contained in the woman.

That is why I also feel that the section of the society that tells women to follow the traditions and customs is afraid of her supremacy. A woman is self-sufficient. It is in her power that the eternal truth of the existence of the universe is contained.

❑

MODERN VIEW OF CULTURE

23.

Vocal for Local

Foundation of Self-Reliant India

The present time is a period of unprecedented circumstances. With Corona, locust attacks, earthquakes as well as negative economic growth for the first time in 41 years, prospect of war on the border with China and Pakistan, there is a battle outside and a war-like situation within. In this challenging environment, Prime Minister Shri Narendra Modi appealed to Indian citizens to purchase local products in order to strengthen the economy. He said that in times of crisis this 'local' has fulfilled our demand, this 'local' has saved us. Local is not just a necessity, it is our responsibility, too.

Being vocal for local products not only promotes the products of Indian companies but also promotes products manufactured in India by multinational companies. The government has emphasized promoting not only products made in India but also local brands, manufacturing, and supply chain. Larger brand acceptance makes the market bigger and also increases the brand valuation. An increase in local productivity will increase employment opportunities, promote a hyper-local market and boost the entire Indian economy in various areas. The success of programs like 'One District, One Program' in Uttar Pradesh, changes in consumer behaviour and inclination towards local products attest to this hypothesis.

The five pillars of *'Atmanirbhar Bharat'* (Self-reliant India) are economy, infrastructure, systems, vibrant demography, and demand. Therefore, the basic spirit of the Hon'ble Prime Minister behind 'Vocal for Local' and 'Self-reliant India' needs to be fully implemented.

Contrary to popular belief, this concept has a long history. Regarding this, Shri. V. D. Savarkar had argued that every step should be taken by the state to protect the national industries against foreign competition. Similarly, Deendayal Upadhyaya had described Swadeshi as an integral element of the philosophy of 'Integral Humanism'.

Datto Pant Thengdi's 'Third Method' provided an alternative to both capitalism and communism. In the long struggle for Indian independence, stalwarts like Dadabhai Naoroji, Bal Gangadhar Tilak (Lokmanya Tilak), Gopal Krishna Gokhale, Mahadev Govind Ranade, and Mahatma Gandhi led the Swadeshi movement. Mahatma Gandhi argued that our villages are on the verge of devastation as the industries had disappeared from the villages. They can be revived only through the revival of rural industries. Subsequently, the Industrial Policy Resolutions of 1948 and 1956 in independent India emphasized the role of rural industries in generating additional employment with low capital investment. Historically, the rural industry has led to increased regional and local capacity building in various sectors, such as Tilonia and Urmul, *Kala Raksha*, *Berojgar Mahila Samiti* (Unemployed Women Committee), etc. in Rajasthan.

Earlier, through the 'Make in India' initiative, an attempt was made to help companies by eliminating barriers to operating in India, due to which the share of manufacturing in the economy increased to 25 percent in 2020 which was 15 percent in 2014. The plan did not succeed much due to the double whammy of rising production costs because of the economic downturn and declining consumption and stricter local regulations. The growth in services and the inherent regional development constraints require a renewed thrust on manufacturing.

The infrastructure problems and institutional constraints faced by the manufacturers have hindered the progress of the value chain. Market infrastructure refers to the institutional infrastructure, which drives productivity by providing infrastructure systems in terms of market information, channels, communication networks, transportation, cold storage, processing, etc., suitable for expanding the delivery of services to the primary, secondary and tertiary sectors.

The Prime Minister emphasized the need for this very vital change at an appropriate time, "At present, we are taking the Indian economy out of 'command and control' state and moving towards 'plug and play'. This is not the time to continue a conservative outlook."

MSMEs, Income Inequality, and Impact on the Military-Industrial Complex

All over the world, especially in developing countries, MSMEs have been the engine of development. The 'Vocal for Local' plan will have a beneficial impact on MSMEs. MSME is the backbone of the Indian economy. It employs approximately 12 crore people. Since MSMEs contribute 34 percent of India's manufacturing output and 45 percent of India's exports, they will help in reducing income inequality by strengthening forward and backward linkages. A recent study conducted by Oxfam showed that the top 1 percent of India's population now owns 73% of the wealth whereas the wealth of 67 crore citizens, comprising half of the country's poorest, increased by only 1 percent between 2006 and 2015. This is sure to boost our military-industrial development complex as well. As of June, 156 Advanced BMP Infantry Combat Vehicles (ICVs) worth Rs 1,094 crore ($145 million) were supplied by state-run ordnance factories in India.

Development and Infrastructural Transformation

There is a need to strengthen the capacity building on a much larger canvas by increasing the capacity of the industries to market their product outside the region. It will expand the economic base of the region; it will maintain the innovative products and processes of the industries to increase both production and productivity to achieve sustainable development both at the regional and national levels.

The Vocal for Local campaign has the potential to expand the scope of industries, such as - Upgradation of industrial infrastructure, the introduction of commercial mining in the coal sector, policy reforms in the mineral sector, policy reforms to increase self-reliance in defence production, nuclear energy reforms and construction of world-class airports through PPP, etc.

Indian companies have proved their mettle by successfully meeting the challenge of instantly ramping up production of essential items like hand sanitizers, ventilators, and masks. Indian brands like Amul, Dabur, Godrej, Tata, etc. do not benefit only because of the sense of pride associated with Indian brands with a diverse, multi-layered consumer group, but also from local media, local language press, social media, and digital platforms. Indian products must focus on quality, innovation, pricing, and marketing mix so that winning the corporate turf war becomes a habit.

For the success of this strategy, a systemic structure for upgrading the market through (a) timely, adequate and low-cost loans, (b) technological up-gradation, (c) vastly improved infrastructure facilities, and (d) demand identification. Up-gradation of skills, and capabilities, optimum utilization of local resources, market research, inter-institutional synergies, committed NGOs and industry associations, good consultants and service providers, etc. are also necessary.

There is a need for an in-depth study of specific groups of developed economies to identify technology gaps and best practices. Clusters can be created at different locations for different products and based on experience, the development model can be replicated in other clusters.

To a large extent, the reality of this campaign depends on the pre-requisites such as the creation of information and marketing network, credit, infrastructure, appropriate technology, JAM Trinity (Jan Dhan-Aadhaar-Mobile) with motivation and training, Direct Benefit Transfer (DBT) and Bank Mitra concept to strengthen Indian ecosystem are necessary. At the same time, a 'mindset' is also required for building competitiveness at the global level.

Given the geopolitical dynamics, complexities of global development, and national requirements, a self-sustaining attitude should be the mantra for success. The new normal requirements are a mission mode to provide level-playing opportunities to our industries and change the ground reality. There is a need for continuous operation of such missions. With the support of all the stakeholders, it can be a game-changer and conceptually change the ground realities.

❑

24.

COVID Diagnosis with Environmental Protection

Environmental protection is the biggest need of the hour for balanced development. As we are running the blind race of materiality, we are also inviting natural and biological calamities. At the core of the dreadful phase of covid that we are all going through right now, the consumerist thinking of development has been prominent. Remember - whenever efforts have been made to speed up development by neglecting nature and life, the whole human race has had to bear the brunt of it. In these times of global pandemic, we need to re-think our *Sanatan* (Traditional) Indian vision of nature conservation in the light of environment-friendly policies along with development. It needs to be kept in mind that the environmental aspect of planning and development should not be omitted. I believe that any scientific development is useful only as long as it does not adversely affect the environment and ecological balance in any way.

Environment means the milieu that surrounds man. Life is completely connected with it. When this circle loses balance, we are faced with Covid and cyclones like Tauktae and Yaas. The *Sanatan* Indian vision has been about worshipping nature. The major scientific fact behind this is that the balance of the ecology should be maintained. Tulsidasji had said long ago in *Ramcharitmanas*, '*Kshiti, jal, pavak, gagan, sameera; panch rachit ati adham sarira.*' But in our pursuit of indiscriminate development and attainment of material achievements, we started neglecting these very five elements associated with the existence of human beings.

I think that the worldwide crisis of the environment that has arisen is due to neglecting the five elements by distancing oneself from nature. Continuing to poison the air and water with chemicals and carbon-emitting gases has led to persistent environmental crises. The reason behind the rapid spread of Covid infection is also environmental imbalance and interfering with the ecosystem.

The destruction of forests has caused the worst damage to the environment. Forest after forest is being destroyed by the rapidly increasing population and comparatively lesser area for the people to live. First Tauktae and then Yaas cyclonic storms are the result of not paying attention to environmental protection. In these times of Covid, there is a lot of discussion about the lack of oxygen. What is the reason for this? We have always taken the matter of Oxygen lightly. Plants and trees are a great source of oxygen. But in consumerist thinking, efforts have been made to bring beauty to homes through new construction by cutting trees, whereas the real adornment of the earth is trees and plants. The more their number reduces, the more the crisis will deepen. It is a scientific fact that trees prevent soil erosion. They recharge groundwater reserves and always create favourable conditions for sustainable agricultural production. So, cutting down trees means disturbing the entire ecosystem. Think about the number of birds, animals and organisms that live on the trees. Due to this biodiversity, balance is maintained in nature. Trees that give shelter to birds grow more trees. I have experienced it myself. There are many species of trees, which grow only from the seeds released by birds.

That is why our culture has a tradition of worshiping trees. In Skanda, Padma Purana, and other ancient texts, it has been said that Brahma resides at the root of the Peepal tree, Vishnu resides in the middle and Lord Shiva resides in the front. Lord Buddha attained enlightenment under the holy Peepal tree.

We have been worshiping the banyan tree as the abode of Shiva. Sadhus and sages carried out their spiritual practices under trees and plants. Why was that? Because the leaves of trees emit positive energy. The mind remains calm near and under the trees.

Khejri is the state tree of Rajasthan. This tree is the everlasting support for the people in the desert and is called *Kalpavriksha* (Tree of heaven). There is a tradition of worshiping it in the form of the *Shami* tree not only in Rajasthan but also across the country. The older generation was wiser than us; they even sacrificed their lives to prevent Khejri from being cut. The sacrifice made for the trees in Khejadli under the leadership of Amrita Devi is the biggest proof of our thinking related to nature conservation embedded in the tree culture.

K. M. Munshi initiated the *Van-Mahotsav* in our country. The country had just become independent and he was the Minister of Food and Agriculture at that time. He understood the importance of trees and started the *Van Mahotsav* by planting saplings in Nainital in 1950. The next year in 1951, he came to Rajasthan and inaugurated a nursery in Jodhpur to prevent the desert from expanding. The tradition of *Van Mahotsav* is continuing even today, but it is not enough. Every person living on the earth should plant a tree and protect it. We have to reduce our needs. It needs to be understood that this earth is not only for us to live on, but it is also for the innumerable organic-inorganic substances, animals and birds, trees and plants, and flora which keep our ecosystem safe. Destruction of trees and vegetation means the destruction of our biodiversity, which results in an imbalance in the environment and a rise in epidemics. Therefore, we must pledge to preserve our culture of nature and the environment. We should embrace the idea of development without disturbing the inherent balance of nature. Remember that trees and plants not only make the land improved and fertile but also sustain everyone.

The real solution to the problems caused by corona lies in nature conservation. Our lives will be prosperous only when we change the consumerist lifestyle and seek development with the thought of renewable energy, eco-friendly construction work, and conserving trees and plants. Only the concepts of eco-friendly development are suitable for the earth and the people living on it. Only then, we can be rid of the future corona-borne disasters, cyclones like Tauktae and Yaas that cause destruction to living beings. Let us take a pledge to work for the entire 365 days of the year and not just one day as Environment Protection Day by staying connected with our *Sanatan* Indian vision of nature conservation.

❑

25.

Industrial Development through Research and Innovations

There is a direct relationship between the industrial development of a country and its economic prosperity. Therefore, it is necessary that in industrial development, along with the adoption of the newest technology, innovations in research and technology should also be adopted. The developed countries of the world like Japan, USA, etc. have done the same. The industrial units there have worked on the strategy of high-development growth by adopting innovations in the development of science and technology as well as industries.

It is very important that India, with the initiative of Prime Minister Shri Narendra Modi, is working on the strategy of future economic development by adopting the latest technology and innovations and making proper use of the available natural resources with the aim of a 'Self-reliant India'.

At present, new opportunities have become available for industries in the research and development-based economy in the country. NITI Aayog has asked all the ministries to spend a certain percentage of their budget on study and research so that the industries can get the benefit of the latest research and innovations over time.

It is a matter of joy for all of us that in September 2020, India was ranked among the 50 leading countries of the world in the Global Innovation Index. This has happened for the first time in history so far. This means that modern India is rapidly moving towards a strong framework of science and technology.

India currently ranks in the top 15 indexes of world companies in information and communication technology, services sector exports, graduates available in science and engineering, online government services, and study and research initiatives. This means that we have a huge field of possibilities in industrial development.

The need is to create a conducive environment for industrial growth by recognizing the availability of our specialization and expertise in various sectors.

In this era of globalization, it is also necessary that all the industries develop an institutionalized system to encourage and drive research and design innovations at their own level. Without this, the country cannot become an important manufacturing power in the industrial sector.

I have also had an opportunity to work in the Ministry of Micro, Small, and Industries of the Government of India. Then, as a Minister in the Ministry of Commerce and Industry, Government of India, we took initiatives like Patent Information Centres, Technology and Innovation Support Centres in the Departments of Science and Technology in states across the country. Organizations like the Confederation of Indian Industry should bring forth entrepreneurs in the states to patent the latest research and designs.

It has been observed that although the latest designs are developed in our country with study and research they are not patented. Considering the importance of patents in the global economy, initiatives should be taken in this regard.

This is because the innovations made by the entrepreneurs at the local level often do not get the platform. Very important products, designs, and research-related elements are, therefore, not recognized on a large scale. Local Centres of Excellence also work as per regional requirements. It is also required that by identifying local innovations, the latest forms of design and research-related areas in such places, the Confederation of Indian Industry should try to bring them forward at their level.

At this time, there is a need to develop such a system in the country which can develop human and technical capability at the level of the enterprise as well as continued promotion of innovations. At this time, there is a need to develop such a system in the country, which can develop human and technical capability in the enterprises as well as continuously encourage innovations. There is no dearth of competence in the country in the field of research and development. But if the development of the main components required for a national research and innovation system is done by the industrial sectors at their level, then its benefits can be reaped at all levels. The costs of market, competencies, availability of skilled labour, and research and development are still very low in our country as compared to other countries.

In the new education policy of the country, special attention has been paid to capacity development keeping professional competence at the centre. Recently, with regard to implementing the new education policy in Rajasthan in practice, I gave more emphasis on the fact that universities should develop such courses so that students can be encouraged for entrepreneurship at the time of getting an education.

The study, research, and innovations have also been given special attention in the new education policy. From this point of view, I believe that at the academic level itself, students should be encouraged to understand and create technology related to objects that are useful in daily life.

In order to promote the trend of innovation and entrepreneurship in the country, along with the establishment of 'Atal Innovation Mission' by NITI Aayog, the main objective of the decisions taken by the Central Government is to establish Atal Tinkering Laboratories across the country for practical training and use of technology is that the country should move towards rapid industrial development. In this regard, the Biotechnology Ignition Grant (BIG) has been started by the Biotechnology Industry Research Assistance Council. This is very important from the point of view of providing grants to young start-ups.

An educated economy is as essential as study, research and innovation are for industrial development. What I mean by an educated economy is that a common understanding of industrial growth is developed at all levels.

A knowledge economy of modern study, research, and innovations can be built rapidly if higher education incorporates courses to develop an understanding of industrial growth and emphasize on vocational skills along with study. The meaning of a knowledge-based economy is to enable sustainable development through science, technology, and modern research and innovations.

The universities across the country are nurseries of knowledge and innovation. If industrial groups spend some percentage of their profit share on education under social responsibility, then industrial development can get its long-term benefits.

❑

26.

Welfare of Migrant Workers is Necessary

The issue of migrant workers has sparked wide-ranging discussions in India's development debate. In the historical and comparative context, migration has given rise to a significant mentality, whereby people are pulling themselves out of the dreadful cycle of poverty. I have had a keen interest in this subject because most of the migration takes place from Uttar Pradesh and Bihar. Chhattisgarh, Jharkhand, Odisha, and Rajasthan are also important sources of migration, where migrant workers depend on jobs related to construction, factory, domestic work, textile, transportation, and farming. Rajasthan, where I work now, is home to a large population of migrants, who are dependent on tourism, production, mining industry, and agriculture for their livelihood. Migration in India is neither a unique phenomenon nor something new. German Chancellor Angela

Merkel predicted in 2015 that the refugee problem would prove to be a defining issue in this decade. In the case of India, it is quite clear from the five-year plan documents and other factual evidence that the issue of migration was not properly taken into account in the development plans and policies. This is surprising because migration affects important aspects like competition, productivity, employment, labour market, and local development. Now with the world undergoing changes after Corona, the discussion on this issue has started intensifying.

Migrant workers in the cities of India are identified on the basis of internal migration, unorganized sector, and seasonal migration. Stiff competition and cost-cutting policies are certain to create dissatisfaction.

Migration is a reality and its pain can be felt. We cannot go back to our old normal lifestyle. We need to pay equal attention to the employment and health of migrant workers. As problems increase, so will the challenges of remodeling this framework, and the need to overhaul the situation of these long-marginalized individuals and groups will also increase. To change the policies affecting their situation, better preparations will have to be made at the quarantine centres by improving the government machinery, especially at the level of primary testing centres. Hence there is a need for a multi-layered initiative.

Unemployment, poverty, and lack of fair employment opportunities are crucial issues at the national level. In 2017-18, out of the total 465 million workers in India, about

91 percent i.e., 422 million workers were employed in the unorganized sector. The 2017 Economic Survey estimated that 139 million of them were seasonal and frequently relocating workers. Migrant workers are residents of rural areas but spend most of the year in cities, where they do not get a regular income. Therefore, the workers involved in the agriculture sector as well as those working in the unorganized sectors may get affected the most. Due to lack of money, many workers had taken shelter in factories that had closed during the lockdown. Apart from this, there is no central registration of migrant workers even though the Inter-State Migrant Workmen (Regulation of Employment and Conditions of Service) Act, 1979 exists. In order to protect the rights of migrant workers and promote welfare, a bill has been introduced in Parliament, namely the Occupational Safety, Health, and Working Conditions Code, 2019. In this code, a proposal has been made to make a law by merging all the 13 labor laws including the 1979 Act.

The lockdown due to Covid-19 has had a negative impact on agriculture, supply chain, food, and nutritional security. There is a shortage of labour in agriculture-intensive states like Punjab, Haryana, Telangana, Maharashtra. Urban areas that have become disease hotspots will face shortages of seasonal labour and there will be economic damage to the construction and manufacturing sectors. These workers will benefit from the 'One Nation One Ration Card' policy, which will help the cardholders to get their quota of food grains even outside their home regions. The implementation of this scheme will be completed by March 2021 and about 67 crore persons will be benefitted. Many demands are being raised to solve the problems concerning the lower class and food shortages faced by the worker class. Some suggestions that are poured in to resolve these issues are incorporating Inter-state cooperation committees to take the workers to their villages, forming judicial cells at the state and central level to solve the problems related to payment of wages, making provision to provide free ration to the migrant workers in urban and industrial areas without any certificate, providing health facilities at the Panchayat level.

Considering the seriousness of this matter, the government has announced several economic policies to reduce the impact on migrant workers. The Finance Minister's second press conference held on 14 May focused on migrant workers, small farmers, and makeshift shopkeepers. He announced a grant of Rs 30,000 crore through NABARD to help small and marginal farmers to grow rabi crops. Even before this, 90 thousand crore rupees have been given under this head. In addition, two crore farmers will be given concessional loans of two lakh crore rupees. 11 thousand crore rupees have been allocated for the poor in urban areas. Migrant workers are also included in this category. With this money, the supply of food and water will be ensured apart from providing shelter to the homeless people. The finance minister expressed concern for migrant workers struggling to go home and raised the rate of wage from ₹ 180 to ₹ 202 per hour. The Central Government has allowed the states to use the State Disaster Relief Fund to provide shelter and food and water to the migrant workers.

For migrant workers, government-funded housing societies will be formed in major cities under the PPP policy, where they will get houses at an affordable rent. There will be a loan facility of five thousand crore rupees for street vendors, which will help 50 lakh, people, to start businesses immediately. The finance minister said that an amount of 10 thousand rupees is being given by the government as initial capital. Eight lakh tonnes of food grains and 50 thousand tonnes of a gram will be given to the states by the central government so that in a month, five kilograms of food grains to every worker and one kilogram of a gram to every family will be given free for two months. Eight crore labourers are expected to benefit from this. This number may go beyond the purview of the National Food Security Act, 2013, and people who have been deprived of this facility so far may also benefit. In view of the enormity of this crisis, many innovative measures have been suggested to fight the epidemic. These include steps like providing affordable housing facilities for migrant workers and urban poor, starting a five thousand crore loan facility for more than 50 lakh makeshift shopkeepers, and using District Mineral Foundation for preparations. These are all important measures in the context of the problem. However, while implementing these, aspects like unusual conditions of the states, intensity of epidemic, availability of facilities, shortage of human resources will have to be considered seriously.

The imperative to focus on migrant workers in India has its roots in the uneven socio-political impact of the pandemic. Therefore, there is a need for the states and the Center to work together as partners in development by strengthening the social security mechanism and facilitating the process of registration. This is a lofty goal and requires a nine-point strategy that has been identified by Dr. Chandrashekhar, Professor, Indira Gandhi Institute of Development Research, Mumbai, and Mukta Nayak, Fellow, Centre for Policy Research, New Delhi –

1. There should be better coordination between states.
2. State Governments should introduce portability within the State and Districts in facilities such as Health Insurance, School Enrollment, and Public Distribution System, as a result of which this facility will eventually be available at the national level as well.
3. State governments should drop the arguments like 'children of the soil', which undermine the freedom to work and reside in any part of the country guaranteed under Article 19 of the Constitution.
4. States should give up the stubbornness of making their official languages a compulsory subject in state government schools.
5. Accounts of rules like the Building and Other Construction Workers (BOCW) Act in each state should be available in all scheduled languages of the country.

6. State governments should officially identify the eligibility of migrant workers, especially construction workers.

7. The registration of migration in the state should be made easy by speeding up the paperwork at the panchayat level.

8. Rental markets and accommodation for migrants and hostels for working men and women should be prepared.

9. The Social Security Code proposal, 2019 should be streamlined to make it more effective.

In order to take swift and effective steps, we have to look at the problem of migrant labour comprehensively. Migrant workers do not have the option of staying at home. If this happens, the most important and vulnerable section of society will stand on the verge of a long-term crisis. We have to create a separate program for living and prepare a mid-term blueprint for development and structural changes. It is a comprehensive framework that will require a review of the national judicial, regulatory, and institutional problems faced in the resettlement of migrant workers. To deal with socio-judicial issues, there is a need to follow human rights-related measures. It is also necessary to resolve the complexities in trade, treasury, currency, and other policies. For example, the implementation of the task force report on migration, participation of migrant women in work like Anganwadi and ANM, admission of migrant children in *Sarva Shiksha Abhiyan* will prove to be effective.

To deal with this serious problem, there is a need to strengthen the financial system and labour policies and programmes. Information and broadcasting technologies and Jan Dhan Aadhar mobile will have to be promoted, which will make it easier to have direct contact with the workers and also reduce the cost. After the physical damage caused by the coronavirus, it has become necessary for all the stakeholders to come together to face the present challenges and live up to the expectations of the future.

❑

27.

Important to Encourage the Micro, Small and Medium Enterprises

The economic situation has collapsed due to the lockdown during the Corona global pandemic. Every sector of the economy has been affected enormously by Covid-19. The backbone of small and medium industries has been broken. The impact of the lockdown on the MSME sector will be visible for a year. It is necessary to seriously contemplate this side effect of lockdown from now itself.

In order to revive the MSME sector, along with giving concessions to it, it is necessary to set criteria for future economic strength. A year after the lockdown due to Covid-19, which is full of worries due to adverse circumstances, will also be a golden opportunity to re-establish small industries.

To re-establish the MSME sector, only a short-term strategy will have to be worked out. Young boys from cities and villages will have to be trained in small-scale industries. Immediate financial assistance will also have to be provided to these youth so that they can re-establish the industries which have been closed for employment. Everyone will have to embrace innovation and technology.

Overall, such an environment has to be created whereby small entrepreneurs can overcome their anxiety and make a fresh start. Entrepreneurs will also have to be mentally prepared to compensate for the losses. For this, the trust and support from the government will work like oxygen for enterprises and small entrepreneurs. This will enable the MSME sector to flourish again.

Banks have to show generosity. The coming year will be full of challenges. In these adverse times, if everyone patiently and seriously extends support to MSMEs, then we will certainly see them emerging in a new form which will bring the economy back on track with renewed vigour and fervour.

With the beginning of the era of economic liberalization, there has been a lot of expansion in the field of entrepreneurship not only in India but all over the world. Entrepreneurship, especially the MSME sector, is making an important contribution to the economy of all developed and developing countries. The contribution of the MSME sector in India is 40 percent in exports, 45 percent in manufacturing, and 8 percent in GDP.

The MSME sector has played an important role in tackling the growing problem of unemployment in the country. The youth can be accommodated and entrepreneurs can be encouraged by expanding the small industries through MSMEs all over the country.

Disruptions in the supply of raw materials and finished goods in the global market will teach us new lessons. These lessons will shape our future. They will prepare the MSME sector to meet the challenges. The strategy prepared after following all these developments will prove to be life-saving for the re-establishment of small and medium industries. This will not only revive the industries that were running before Covid-19, but it will also create an environment for new industries. This will be a new environment for India. It will also give new opportunities to small industries to flourish.

Global companies are exploring other countries to diversify their manufacturing and supply chains to avoid risks. There are a lot of opportunities for setting up manufacturing facilities in India. Top companies from the US and Japan have already started exiting China. India should take advantage of this by streamlining the infrastructure, quality of labour, and policy framework.

The government should ensure that there is no disruption in the global supply chain. With its industrial network, abundant natural resources, and relatively cheap workforce, India can attract global manufacturers as an alternative base.

India can present itself as a credible option to increase its share of textile and apparel exports. Brand diversification strategy is essential in the post-corona era. In the future, in view of any situation like the corona global epidemic, our dependence on China will have to be reduced.

India should not underestimate itself. India has immense potential. India's youth have energy. India has to explore new opportunities to promote entrepreneurs in promising sectors like minerals, metals, homeware, ceramic tiles, engineering goods, furniture, etc.

Rapid digitization of services will help the stakeholders to access those services seamlessly. This includes the digital transformation of enterprises along with telecom operators, smartphones and their associated ecosystems, online gaming and streaming content, the use of robots in assembly-line production, cloud computing, assistive devices, and remote working capabilities.

Reverse migration of labour will encourage light industries in the villages, especially in the food processing industry. India is the second-largest producer of fruits and vegetables. With a proper start-up ecosystem i.e., electricity, water, connectivity of roads, marketing, technology, modernization, and regular supply of credit, start-ups must be encouraged to develop cold chain logistics.

There is no doubt that in the post-corona period, small industries will get a new lease of life. This will be revolutionary for MSMEs. There will be a rise in employment. The economy will be strengthened. Every village will be prosperous. Along with agriculture, small industries will be more successful in changing the condition and giving a new direction to the life of our fellow citizens.

In the present situation, the highest priority of the State Government is to bring the affected economy back on track. For this, there should have been the availability of cash along with a solid arrangement of funds for essential services so that they can meet their minimum needs. The state government should provide three months of relaxation in the utility cost for the urban poor so that the financial pressure on them can be reduced. Similarly, there is a need to provide exemption in local taxes in selected areas by the state government.

Similarly, after the lockdown, the government should prepare a plan for logistics management in the industry sector, especially by encouraging small-scale industries, controlling operational expenses, undertaking labour management and promoting liquidity logistics in the market.

Not only this, the state government, in collaboration with the private sector, needs to provide support for large quantities of low-cost sanitizers, masks, testing kits, and other preventive measures. With this, the means of prevention will be easily available to the general public, especially health workers.

At this time of the global pandemic, when not only states but the entire nation is passing through a difficult phase, central and state governments, doctors, health personnel administration, policymakers need to do everything possible to face this challenge and make concerted efforts to overcome it.

❑

28.

Timely Initiative by a Self-Reliant Nation

Covid-19 has had a massive impact on the world economy. The present times are dire and the situation is quite worrisome. Every country has taken necessary steps from the political and economic points of view to deal with this disaster. India is also constantly trying to deal with this disaster.

In this time of serious crisis, Prime Minister Shri Narendra Modi presented a vision document of self-reliant India on 12th May, on the basis of which Finance Minister Smt. Nirmala Sitharaman presented an economic package of 20 lakh crores from 13th May to 16th May, which is about 10 percent of India's GDP. This package is based on the five pillars of self-reliant India, namely - Economy,

Infrastructure Development, System, Entrepreneurial Population, and Demand. These five bases will strengthen India's economy as well as establish India as a self-reliant nation at the international level. This economic package will help strengthen various sectors of the country as well as in re-establishing cottage industries, micro, small and medium enterprises, workers, middle class, and industries.

This package will cater to the needs of almost all sections of the country. This package is for cottage industries, micro, small and medium enterprises, labourers, middle class. In the present context, there cannot be a better package than this to give new energy to the country. This package will definitely increase the self-reliance of the country and will promote local to global products. This package is effective for today's India. This will make the country dynamic to move forward by improving the conditions at the ground level. It will also be beneficial in the process and pattern of development for those who are marginalized.

The economic stimulus package was announced on 26 March by the Government of India and the Reserve Bank of India, in line with the immediate and undetermined monetary policy on 27 March and another monetary policy announced on 17 April. These policy announcements supported by this package would definitely be effective in bringing the economy on the right track. While this comprehensive policy includes exemption for employers and employees of all establishments registered with EPFO, on the other hand a special liquidity scheme of thirty thousand crores for non-banking financial companies, housing finance companies and micro-finance institutions is also included.

A provision of a partial credit guarantee scheme of Rs 45,000 crore has also been made for the liabilities of non-banking financial companies and micro-finance institutions. Providing liquidity of 90 thousand crore rupees for DISCOMs, relief to contractors and real estate, exemption on goods covered by direct taxes and heavy emphasis on micro, small and medium industries are the main points of this economic package.

Arrangements have been made for 1.70 lakh crore for Pradhan Mantri Garib Kalyan Yojana and up to 60 percent advance by the Reserve Bank of India to state governments, ensuring additional liquidity of Rs 1.37 lakh crore by reducing CRR and special refinancing for NABARD, SIDBI, and NHB. Announcement of short-term and long-term measures to help the poor including migrant labourers, farmers, small traders, street vendors, and important measures for strengthening agriculture, fisheries, food processing, agricultural infrastructure sectors, capacity building, and governance, and administrative reforms has also been included in this package.

The Micro, Small, and Medium Enterprises (MSMEs) are a huge conglomerate of about 63 million units, which account for 30 percent of India's GDP and 45 percent of manufacturing. With regard to employment, after agriculture, MSMEs employ the largest number of people which is about 11 crore people. In the present scenario, the position of micro, small and medium enterprises has somewhat weakened. The resilience of this sector is less in the circumstances arising due to the rapidly growing global economy. But through *'Atmnirbhar Bharat'* (Self-reliant India), the time has come that with the motto of *'Vasudhaiv Kutumbakam'* we will be able to establish these local micro, small and medium enterprises into global ones.

There are more than 60 definitions of micro, small and medium enterprises in 75 countries. The main parameters of the definitions are based on the size of employment, capital investment, fixed assets, etc. Small and medium enterprises in the European Union countries are considered to have less than 500 employees, while in East Asia enterprises with 50-100 workers are considered small and medium. In order to create a competitive and healthy environment in our country, the investment limit in plants and machinery has been increased. The turnover criterion, which is an important point for evaluating creditworthiness by banks and financial institutions, has also been prescribed as one of the key parameters for availing of cheap and accessible loans.

Some start-ups, which have closed down and meet the criteria of the changed definition of micro, small and medium enterprises, may also get the benefit of liquidity along with fiscal and other benefits. The format of the altered definition of Micro, Small, and Medium Enterprises has changed now. In the changed format, the investment limit of up to one crore in micro-enterprise and turnover of 5 crores, investment limit of 10 crores in small enterprise and turnover of 50 crores, investment limit of 20 crores in medium enterprise and turnover of 100 crores has been kept. Thus, the distinction between manufacturing and service sector has been obliterated by including a very important parameter of turnover in the definitions of micro, small and medium enterprises.

Approximately 90 percent of the total formal credit to micro, small and medium enterprises is funded by banks and 10 percent by non-banking financial institutions. Of the total Rs. 15 lakh crore of formal credit given to micro, small and medium enterprises, nearly one-third is less than ₹ 1 crore. In the last several years, the NPA of MSMEs is also only 4 to 8 percent, whereas the average NPA of other enterprises is 15 to 18 percent. But the micro, small and medium industries have not been supported by the banks due to various reasons. Liquidity and liquidity constraints remain the biggest concern for micro, small and medium enterprises during this difficult period of COVID-19. In the present scenario, the growth and stability of MSMEs will determine the direction of development and progress of the country. Accordingly, in the economic package announced by the finance minister on May 13, along with increasing the liquidity, another important step has also been taken.

For businesses including micro, small and medium enterprises, a provision of a collateral free automatic loan of ₹ 3 lakh crore has been made. This will benefit about 45 lakh entrepreneurs. This relief will be available for units with outstanding loans up to ₹ 25 crore and a turnover of ₹ 100 crore. These units will not have to give any guarantee or security. The Government of India will give a 100 percent guarantee for these amounts. There is also a provision of giving a moratorium of 12 months on the payment of the principal amount. The benefit of this scheme can be taken till October 31, 2020.

The government has made a provision of subsidy loan of 20 thousand crores for those two lakh micro, small and medium enterprises, which are struggling with NPAs or are burdened with debt.

The government will provide the necessary support to the Credit Guarantee Trust for Micro and Small Enterprises (CGTMSE) by giving ₹ 4,000 crore. Banks are expected to provide subsidy credit to such units which are contributing to the promotion of MSMEs and their share in the concerned unit is equal to 15 percent. This loan will be up to maximum of ₹ 75 lakh. The benefit of this system of subsidy credit should also be provided to the healthy micro, small and medium industries of the past. With this, in the coming times, the industries burdened with debt due to Covid-19 will be able to be debt-free. Banks will now be able to play a more effective role in the revival and restoration of MSMEs as arrangements have been made by the government to provide them with refinancing benefits while providing them with more liquidity. Guidelines in this regard have been issued by the Reserve Bank of India in 2015 itself.

Micro, small and medium industries face an acute shortages of equity. Therefore, the government will set up a Fund of Funds with a corpus of 10 thousand crores, which will provide equity funding support to micro, small and medium enterprises. The Fund of Funds will operate through a composite fund and a few subsidiary funds. With the measures taken by the government, equity of about 50 thousand crore rupees will be raised in the Fund of Funds. This will help MSMEs to expand in size and capacity and they will also get an opportunity to get listed on the main board of stock exchanges.

Global tender is not considered in the purchase of goods and services worth less than 200 crores. This will allow MSMEs to be more competitive in government procurement and supply.

E-market linkage will be promoted for micro, small and medium enterprises, which will replace the trade fairs and exhibitions held earlier. MSMEs will be paid by the government and public sector undertakings in 45 days. This is extremely important as earlier most of the MSMEs faced many difficulties in getting their payment even in 90 days.

There is also an important suggestion that MSMEs who were not using the credit facilities of the bank and whose condition is not good at present, may be considered for benefits similar to Mudra Yojana.

Today the whole world is facing a crisis. In the past, we have not faced this type of adversity, but we have faced other kinds of adversities and odd situations determinedly. We have won through confidence, dedication, perseverance, and achievement of the set goals. From this crisis, we will move ahead by making MSMEs helmsman, as written by Ramdhari Singh 'Dinkar' Ji –

Senani! Karo prayan Abhay
Bhavi itihas tumhara hai
Yeh nakhat ama ke bujhate hain
Sara akasha tumhara hai.

We Indians, believing in our innate dynamism and potential, have to continuously move the wheel of development considering all innovations and all-new options so that with revived growth and innovation, we can successfully meet the challenges of today and be able to meet the expectations of tomorrow.

With these efforts of the government, the economic base of the country will expand and the future will continue the tradition of sustainable development through MSMEs, cottage industries, and new products and innovations. The current policy of the government is also important because it will help in achieving sustainable growth and development both at the regional and national levels without increasing the fiscal deficit.

During this phase, first of all, we should not let our faith be shaken and we should also drive away fear from the mind. This policy/economic package will definitely drive away from the feeling of fear from inside us. We will succeed. This unfavourable time shall pass. Into a new dawn, shall we awaken!

❑

29.

Disregard for Tribals and Naxalism

Naxalism is the biggest problem of the current time. The biggest threat to the internal security of the country is believed to be from the Naxalites. According to a rough estimate, Naxalism is not only causing loss of life and property at many levels in the country, but by tricking the youth of the country, it is also putting a question mark on their future. Due to Naxalism, the Indian Army has suffered continuous losses within the country rather than on the border.

It is believed that the activities of Naxalites (Maoists) in the country are allegedly being carried out against the exploitation of the tribals. According to a rough estimate, the Naxalites have captured an area of about 40,000 square kilometres and about 2000 police stations. Naxalism is considered to be the exploitation of tribals directly or indirectly and separation from the mainstream of the country.

History is witness that the tribals have been an integral part of our society. Lord Rama had received a lot of help from the Kol and Bhil tribesmen in his conquest of Lanka. Similarly, Alexander had to face tough opposition from tribal groups in the northwest before the battle with Porus. Probably because of this, Alexander returned to his country after the war with Porus. In the first war of independence in 1857, the tribals had supported Maharani Laxmibai against the British. Why did these tribals move away from the mainstream of society over a period of time? This is a matter of concern for the entire Indian society.

According to the 2001 census, there are 8.2 percent tribals in the country, in which there are about 698 races. They speak 106 languages and live in about 19 states and 6 union territories. Their exploitation started from the British Imperialism era and continued indirectly till the 90s in independent India, the result of which the country is suffering in the form of Naxalism (Maoist). In 1950, the tribals were added to the list of sub-constitution of the Scheduled Tribes to provide them constitutional protection and security so that their economic development could take place. But due to the lack of willpower of the government, the result was zero.

In 1999, during the NDA rule, a national policy for the development of tribal areas was formulated. In the year 2003, Tribal Cooperative Marketing Development

Federation (TCMDF) was formed to procure tribal products like honey, rope, jute, leaves, bamboo products, etc. for the welfare of tribals. In 2002, during the NDA regime, the National Commission for Scheduled Tribes was formed by the 89th amendment of the Constitution so that the tribals could be provided with education, health, employment and they could be included in the mainstream of the nation. But in 2005, the government added fuel to the fire by bringing controversial bills like the Scheduled Tribes (Recognition of Forest Rights) Bill 2005. Under this bill, many restrictions regarding the use of forests were imposed on the indigenous people whereas the deforestation continued with the collusion between the officials and the forest land mafia, and natural resources continued to be exploited. During British imperialism, the foundation for the exploitation of tribals was laid in 1871 through the Criminal Tribe Act 187. Through this act, 200 tribal communities were declared heritage criminals. Initially, this act was implemented only in North India. Surprisingly, there were no proper protests against this inhuman act. This black law was abolished in 1952, 5 years after independence. Many movements were launched by the tribals against British rule. Some of these were against economic exploitation and some were against restrictions on the use of forests. But after independence, the tribal movements can be mainly divided into three parts-

- Movement against the exploitation of the Santhal and Munda races and local tribals by outsiders.
- Movement by the Gonds of Madhya Pradesh and the Mahars of Andhra Pradesh against the denial of opportunities for economic progress.

- Agitation due to the different tendencies of Nagas and Bhijs.

Thus, today's tribal movement, which has been given a different form by the Maoists due to their vested interests, started only because of economic exploitation by outsiders and not getting an opportunity for economic development. In the social sector too, due to the acquisition of natural resources by private companies, the problems of poverty, hunger, unemployment increased among the tribals, and they were heavily exploited by outsiders.

Adivasis are being exploited for the last 150 years. They have been isolated from the mainstream of the nation. There is still a contradiction in the government about solving this problem. The home minister does not want to talk to Maoists, another cabinet minister addressed a rally supported by Maoists. In view of the elections in Orissa, the Congress General Secretary calling himself the biggest well-wisher of the tribals declared himself their soldier. Is the Government of India unaware that it took 52 years i.e., till the year 1999 to announce the National Policy for the tribals and to form the Tribal Ministry for them? In the tribal areas, there was an exploitation of natural resources and indiscriminate deforestation. Maoist organizations are using simple tribal people for their personal gain. They do not want solutions to the problems of the tribals. Incidents of killing and abducting innocent police personnel are immoral and condemnable. If the government wants the tribals to have confidence in the government, then the following steps should be taken-

- In the year 2003, the Tribal Cooperative Marketing Development Federation was formed for the marketing of honey, rope, jute, leaves, etc. produced by the tribals. It should be extended to all tribal areas.
- Special projects should be started for the rehabilitation, education, health, and poverty alleviation of the tribals and protection of their language and those projects should be implemented in a time-bound manner. Only by helping to heal the wounds that have been affecting the tribals for almost 150 years can they be included in the mainstream of the nation.
- There are school buildings in tribal areas, but no teachers. In some schools, children study outside and the police use the school building. The government will have to make arrangements for education in the tribal areas smoothly. Only education and economic development can save us from the problem.

❑❑❑